Integrating Children's Literature and Mathematics in the Classroom

Children as Meaning Makers, Problem Solvers, and Literary Critics

Integrating Children's Literature and Mathematics in the Classroom

CHILDREN AS MEANING MAKERS, PROBLEM SOLVERS, AND LITERARY CRITICS

Michael Schiro

Teachers College, Columbia University
New York and London

Published by Teachers College Press, 1234 Amsterdam Avenue, New York, NY 10027

Library of Congress Cataloging-in-Publication Data
Schiro, Michael.
    Integrating children's literature and mathematics in the classroom
: children as meaning makers, problem solvers, and literary critics
/ Michael Schiro.
       p.   cm.
    Includes bibliographical references (p.) and index.
    ISBN 0-8077-3565-5 (alk paper). — ISBN 0-8077-3564-7 (pbk. :
alk. paper)
    1. Mathematics—Study and teaching (Elementary)   2. Children's
literature in mathematics education. I. Title.
QA135.5.S284   1996
372.7'044—dc20   96-33604

ISBN 0-8077-3564-7 (paper)
ISBN 0-8077-3565-5 (cloth)
Printed on acid-free paper
Manufactured in the United States of America
04 03 02 01 00 99 98 97   8 7 6 5 4 3 2 1

Contents

Preface

Several years ago I ran a simple errand—going to a nearby bookstore to purchase children's trade books that related to mathematics—that led to an extraordinary adventure in exploring some of the relationships between mathematics, children's literature, and literary criticism. This book is about two parts of that adventure: my search for ways of using trade books to provide children and educators with powerful instructional experiences that integrate the study of mathematics and children's literature, and my search for excellent children's trade books that contain mathematics.

The book's introductory chapter describes reasons for integrating the study of mathematics and children's literature as well as the history of my search for excellent children's mathematics trade books and powerful instructional methods of using them.

Chapter 2 presents a classroom example of an instructional method that helps children and adults better understand mathematics, literature, and themselves.

Chapter 3 examines the philosophical and pedagogical underpinnings of the instructional model presented in Chapter 2.

Chapter 4 discusses standards useful in assessing children's mathematics trade books. It will sensitize the reader to the strengths and weaknesses of such books and provide the vocabulary necessary for insightfully discussing them.

Chapter 5 explores ways of mathematically enhancing children's books to enrich their reader's mathematical and literary experiences.

The appendix provides an assessment instrument useful for evaluating children's mathematics trade books.

This book should elevate the quality of the current discussion about the connection between mathematics and children's literature. It should aid educators who want to select and use children's trade books, mathematics and literacy educators who wish to explore relationships between mathematics and literature study, authors who want to write excellent children's mathematics books, and publishers who must review and edit children's books.

Readers who are primarily interested in the ways in which trade books can be evaluated and mathematically enriched should probably read Chapters 4 and 5 first, before proceeding to the first two chapters.

Educators who work with teachers or other adults can have them read Chapter 4, examine children's books, read Chapter 5, engage in mathematical literary criticism and editing themselves using a book such as *The Doorbell Rang* (Hutchins, 1986), and then read Chapters 2 and 3 to gain increased insight into the instructional process.

A decision had to be made about which children's books to include in this study. In general, any book that has a plot built around a mathematical concept or that directly poses a mathematical problem to its characters or the reader is considered to contain mathematics. The mathematical concepts underlying books can be wide-ranging and include those of classification, numeration, place value, counting, arithmetic operations, fractions, geometry, measurement, or logic. One important category of book is not included in this study, however: those that a mathematically inclined person could build a mathematics problem around even though no mathematics is contained in the book. Those who love mathematics see it everywhere and can turn almost any book into a mathematical exploration: If a person owns three hats, one can ask how many different ways they can be stacked; if a book's characters play a dice game, one can examine dice probability; if a book contains words, one can even estimate and then count them. For the mathematically inclined, mathematics is everywhere. This is as it should be for all of us. While recognizing that mathematics is everywhere, this study focuses only on children's books that actually contain mathematics—either underlying their story or in problems they pose for their characters or readers.

Special credit needs to be given to Karen Bell, Karen Braatvedt, Rainy Cotti, Joann Greenwood, Pamela Halpern, Pat Heimgartner, Patricia Howson, Doris Lawson, Fran Loftus, and Christine Moynihan. Thank you for joining the journey that led to the writing of this book.

Integrating
Children's Literature
and Mathematics
in the Classroom

Children as Meaning Makers, Problem Solvers, and Literary Critics

1

Introduction

The National Council of Teachers of Mathematics (NCTM) recently declared that one of the major goals of school mathematics should be to increase the amount and quality of children's mathematical communication (1989). This has motivated many teachers to use children's books as a vehicle for facilitating and enhancing the communication of mathematical ideas. Recent interest in the "whole language" approach to reading, "literature based" language arts, and "reading across the disciplines" has also led many educators to use children's literature as a vehicle for enriching and giving meaning to the school mathematics curriculum.

In support of these endeavors educators have published books that describe how to use children's literature to help teach mathematics, including *How to Use Children's Literature to Teach Mathematics* (Welchman-Tischler, 1992), *Math and Literature* (Burns, 1992b), *Math Through Children's Literature* (Braddon, Hall, & Taylor, 1993), and *It's the Story That Counts* (Whitin & Wilde, 1995). At the same time, teachers are searching for children's trade books useful in teaching mathematics, conference presentations on linking mathematics and literature have become popular, educational materials supply houses are aggressively promoting trade books that contain mathematics, and some mathematics textbook series are beginning to incorporate children's literature in student texts, supplementary readings, and teacher's manuals.

The movement to use children's literature to facilitate the teaching of mathematics is well underway, and out of this movement is emerging another newer trend—integrating the teaching of mathematics and literature in a way that helps children simultaneously learn both subjects. This book has grown out of an inquiry into that approach, which is described below. In order to provide perspective on the book's place in the fields of mathematics education and language arts instruction, the introduction also will discuss the relationship of this study to other educators' endeavors to integrate the teaching of mathematics and literature.

1

ORIGIN OF THE STUDY

In 1988 I obtained money to purchase children's trade books related to mathematics for my curriculum library. I went to a nearby bookstore and bought every children's mathematics book that I could find. I also ordered books that were reviewed in journals, advertised in catalogs, described in annotated bibliographies, and recommended by educators and librarians. I let them accumulate for a while before taking the time to carefully examine my collection.

What a disappointment! A few of the books were excellent, but I also acquired a large number of books with incorrect or confusing mathematics, boring books, books with missed opportunities to highlight mathematics, and books with mathematics whose difficulty levels were not matched to the interest levels of their illustrations, story, and vocabulary.

In an effort to understand why I was finding so few excellent books, I searched for standards useful in assessing the quality of children's mathematics trade books. I examined many publications—including bibliographies, journals, and book reviews—and could find no standards that were rigorous or carefully conceived.

Evaluation Standards

Since no comprehensive set of standards seemed to exist, I decided to create my own. By 1990 I generated a set of mathematical standards and a set of literary standards for excellent children's mathematics trade books, along with subordinate criteria that defined each standard. I soon realized, however, that I didn't have enough time available to further develop both sets of standards and that I would have to restrict my focus to just one. I chose mathematical standards because little had been written on the subject, whereas much was already written about children's literary criticism. Moreover, while many journals review generic children's books and numerous organizations give awards for generic children's literature, such journals and awards do not exist for children's literature containing mathematics.

I created the first of many drafts of an assessment instrument based on the mathematical standards and assembled a study group of educators to field test it. The study group's purpose was to discuss children's mathematics trade books while using my assessment instrument to rate those books from excellent to poor.

Within a year, the study group evolved to include a university mathematics educator, a university early childhood educator, two school district mathematics coordinators, two remedial reading teachers, two regular classroom teachers, and one elementary school mathematics specialist, most of whom had young school aged children of their own. This allowed the group to examine books from the perspectives of both professional educators and parents. Prior to the study group discussion, books evaluated with the assessment instrument were often used both in classrooms and homes.

As the study group met, the evaluation instrument was revised many times. My initial focus had been on a detailed analysis of the mathematical components of children's trade books that would permit ranking the books and provide a solid basis for justifying both the analyses and the rankings. I started with a 14-page instrument that contained 13 mathematical standards, each of which was defined by numerous specific criteria. In time, after study group members complained about the tedium of using such a detailed assessment instrument, several standards were merged and a short 1-page instrument developed.

However, as I began to work with educators outside of the study group, I became dissatisfied because the short instrument allowed books to be evaluated without describing the reasons for the assessments. I now wanted more from my assessment instrument than simply the ability to reliably rank books: I wanted it to help educators develop their own critical analytical perspectives with which to view books. I therefore developed a 3-page assessment instrument that balanced book assessment with fostering the development of analytical skills and perspectives; the long instrument was used only as part of training sessions.

Over time I observed that educators' developing analytical skills spontaneously spread from assessing the mathematical dimensions of books to assessing literary dimensions, and I became more interested in the integration of mathematical and literary endeavors. In 1993, returning to the literary standards I had initially developed and then abandoned, I devised a 2-page assessment instrument and merged it with the mathematical instrument. The resulting 5-page instrument is designed to encourage the development of the reviewers' own critical literary and mathematical perspectives as they assess both the mathematical and literary dimensions of children's mathematics trade books.

Integration of Mathematics and Literature Instruction

As the group's thinking and discussions matured over time, its focus changed. Initially the focus had been on *using* my assessment instrument to evaluate and rate books in relation to the standards as we attempted to *understand* both their mathematics and how well books presented it. By 1992, the focus shifted toward *refining* the instrument while we searched for books' mathematics and *devised plans* for rewriting books to better clarify and present their mathematics that capitalized upon their strengths and compensated for their weaknesses. The shift in emphasis occurred because as the members of the group developed the ability to see the strengths and weaknesses of books they were naturally led to formulate ways in which books could be improved.

As the study group continued to meet, we began to replicate with our students the type of mathematical literary criticism that we engaged in ourselves. Doris, a group member who taught fourth grade, rewrote the assessment instrument for students and had them use it to evaluate children's books. Doris thought that mathematical standards would be easier to use than literary standards, and that she could teach the process of literary criticism more easily by focusing on mathematical issues rather than literary issues—children, she assumed, would be able to more easily answer questions about such things as the accuracy of mathematics in children's books than such things as how well developed and imaginative a book's plot was. Doris discovered that two activities—examining children's books to discover their mathematics and assessing both the meaning of that mathematics and the adequacy of its presentation—were major problem-solving endeavors for her students. Searching for the existence of mathematics was an "open-ended" task in which her students themselves found books' mathematical problems. Once children discovered a book's problems, they were naturally drawn into a discussion that clarified the nature of those problems, the mathematical algorithms that could be used to solve them, the meaning of the mathematics that was used in the algorithms, and the adequacy of the book's presentation of its mathematics. For Doris, helping her students become mathematical literary critics involved first discovering mathematical problems in books and then understanding both the nature of the mathematics related to those problems and the adequacy of a book's presentation of its mathematics.

Joanne—a member of the study group who taught fifth and sixth graders—re-enacted mathematical literary criticism with her students in a different way. Joanne and her school librarian jointly presented *The Pushcart War* (Merrill, 1964) to their students. The librarian, who initially did not think the book contained mathematics, read the book and discussed its literary dimensions with the children, one chapter at a sitting. After each reading and discussion of a chapter by the school librarian, Joanne re-examined that same reading with her students to discover if it presented any mathematics. She and her students discovered "hidden" mathematics that they had not previously seen, worked through the calculations it involved, questioned its meaning and contextual reasonableness, and assessed the adequacy of the book's presentation of its mathematics. (Part of the charm of *The Pushcart War* is that its mathematics does not always make sense once one does the calculations.) After much discussion of the book's mathematics and the adequacy of its presentation, Joanne, the school librarian, and the students decided to rewrite the book as a play. In their script they invented a "mathematical commentator," who explained the mathematics occurring within the play to the audience. This is an important mathematical element that is not in the original version of the book. The play was written and successfully performed for the school.

Joanne and Doris started at the same place and discussed their endeavors on a regular basis, but the two educators ended up going on very different mathematical adventures and discovering some very different things about the process of mathematical literary criticism. Joanne had students "acting as mathematicians" as they

1. Searched for a book's mathematics
2. Clarified the nature of that mathematics
3. Checked its meaning, reasonableness, application, and solutions
4. Discussed how adequately the book presented its mathematics
5. *Devised a plan* to rewrite the book as a dramatic play so that they could better present its mathematics
6. *Carried out the plan* by producing the play

One difference between Joanne's and Doris' approach is that Joanne had children "act and think as though they were mathematicians." Another difference is that Joanne's children went beyond *discovering* problems and *understanding* a book's mathematics and the effectiveness of its presentation, to *devising a plan* to improve the book, and *carrying out the plan*. What was emerging was a somewhat enriched parallel structure to that of Polya's (1957) four-stage scheme for approaching problem solving in a systematic manner: understand the problem, devise a plan for solving it, carry out the plan, and look back to see what was accomplished.

Kareen—a study group member who taught second grade—took her students on a different adventure in mathematical literary criticism. She first read books to her students and then had them both search for the books' mathematics and evaluate its correctness. The students were delighted with the treasure hunt for "hidden" mathematics, thrilled to discover that adults made mathematical mistakes in their published books, and very active discussants of the meaning of the mathematics they discovered as they explained and justified why that mathematics might or might not be correct. From the outset, Kareen made group discussion a central part of using mathematical literary criticism with her students, thus fostering mathematical communication among the children in her class. As Kareen continued the process, she asked her students to turn their attention to how effectively the books presented their mathematics. This led to discussions of alternate ways of presenting a book's mathematics and representing its mathematical meanings (i.e., in the form of written words, diagrams, graphs, pictures, algorithms, equations, etc.). Finally, Kareen's students proposed revisions for the books, made plans for rewriting them, actually rewrote them, and then discussed their endeavors.

Devising a plan to solve a problem is not the same as carrying out the plan. In our study group we only devised plans for improving children's books, but Kareen's second graders took two additional steps. First her students rewrote books in the different ways that they each thought best. Then they displayed their rewritten books along with the original published books so that they could examine, assess, and discuss the adequacy of their own solutions, their classmates' solutions, and the original author's solution to the core problem: presenting the book's mathematics in the most effective, meaningful, artistic, and pleasing manner. By taking these two additional steps, Kareen completed the problem-solving process suggested by Polya: understand the problem, devise a plan, carry out the plan, and look back to see the adequacy of the solution and the transferability of the plan.

The study group did not plan to discover a new type of problem solving that children could engage in. The meaning of what we accomplished only emerged as we pursued our exploration of what it meant to have children engage in "mathematical literary criticism." This required a conceptual framework within which those accomplishments could be considered, some new language to discuss what we accomplished, and some time to look back and reflect on both the "problem" we solved through our actions and the "solution" we proposed.

A critical part of the analysis of our endeavor was the discovery that we had invented a well-defined instructional procedure, which we termed *mathematical literary criticism*: "the process of examining children's books with respect to a set of mathematical standards." That definition was exceeded, however, when we began having children actually rewrite commercial trade books, editing and redesigning books but leaving the original story intact. We couldn't quite call the children "authors" in this case, so we settled on "mathematical editor," even though they were being asked to do much more than simply "edit" books.

In addition to making the children mathematical literary critics and editors, we were also asking them to act and think as mathematicians as they engaged in open-ended problem solving. Discovering the similarity between what we invented and what mathematics educators interpret as Polya's paradigm for systematically approaching mathematical problems was a major breakthrough: Essentially, we had expanded Polya's four-phase approach to include a new initial step, having children discover problems. Mathematics problems thus become conceptualized as situations in which one finds, clarifies, and communicates to others mathematical meanings, rather than situations in which one simply solves problems. We also realized that what we were doing fully accorded with having children engage mathematics as problem solving, reasoning, communication, and connections, as suggested in the four common standards in *Curriculum And Evaluation Standards For School Mathematics* (NCTM, 1989).

Based on the study group members' work with children, I introduced mathematical literary criticism and editing to a group of experienced elementary school teachers during a summer course I taught. I presented mathematical standards, demonstrated how to evaluate the mathematical components of children's books, and suggested a few ways of enhancing children's books. Once they overcame their initial resistance to altering a published children's book, the teachers were very productive. They found ways of transforming *The Doorbell Rang* (Hutchins, 1986) into a learning experience suitable for first through sixth graders. First and second grade teachers adapted the book to deal with addition, subtraction, and measurement; third and fourth grade teachers used it to explore division, multiplication, and geometric patterns; and fifth and sixth grade teachers were excited about its potential to present fractions and ratios. The teachers' analyses of the book surpassed those of children, but teachers and children both discovered the same mathematical inadequacies with the book. The teachers were far more capable than the children of carrying out their planned enhancements, and they invented numerous ways of improving children's books. The process of conceiving and creating these changes was critical in helping the teachers to see themselves as powerful mathematical and literary agents. The teachers said that acting as a mathematical literary critic and editor was easier than they had expected, and the opportunity to knowledgeably critique and actually alter books to make them more vital pieces of literature was empowering. Overall, the experience changed their conceptions of how children, teachers, and books could interact.

These teachers in my class also asked me why we were not focusing on the *literary* dimensions of the books as well as their mathematics, and they strongly urged me to expand into this area. I considered their request during the remainder of the summer.

The next year Karen and Rainy—two mathematics educators working with preservice teachers—joined the study group. The three of us decided to teach mathematical literary criticism and editing to our undergraduate and graduate preservice teachers. In an effort to introduce literary issues to the process, I created a new assessment instrument that contained both mathematical and literary standards. While we only presented mathematical standards, assessment perspectives, and enhancement techniques, we watched carefully to see what the preservice teachers would do with the literary standards. They started out with mathematical observations and plans for how to mathematically enhance books. However, during the process of mathematical literary criticism and editing they showed an increased awareness of how mathematical changes could affect the literary dimensions of a book and vice versa. Every preservice teacher had insights into the literary dimensions of the books they were working on and almost everyone enhanced literary components of their books. Some literary enhancements were minor, involving only issues of language; others were major and involved rewriting books to remedy perceived inadequacies in a book's plot or characterization.

While I was working with these preservice teachers, I asked several elementary school teachers to try integrating mathematical and literary analysis of children's books with their students. Their reports on the experience emphasized three findings. First, mathematical literary criticism and editing was considerably easier for their students than its purely literary counterpart. Evidently, analyzing such literary elements as plot, characterization, and language was more difficult for children than dealing with the presentation of mathematical topics, and the students seemed to find altering a book's literary elements more taxing than editing the presentation of its mathematical ideas. Second, working initially with mathematical literary criticism and editing seemed to provide children with an intellectual perspective on literary criticism and a sense of literary power that facilitated their analysis of a book's literary dimensions. The children seemed to enjoy making suggestions for improving the literary dimensions of books, even though most seemed to lack the ability to translate their suggestions into action that actually transformed a book. Third, after engaging in mathematical literary criticism and editing, children seemed to be more receptive to analyzing and editing their own writing. This seemed to make sense, for if children develop a frame of mind that leads them to analyze and enhance books, then that intellectual perspective should be transferable to their own writing.

These were delightful findings. Almost all the benefits of linking mathematics and literature discussed in the professional literature were one directional: Teachers used children's books to help children engage in mathematics; children's books were used primarily as a tool to stimulate mathematical thinking, and there was little vision of how to integrate literature and mathematical study so that students developed their literary and mathematical abilities simultaneously. Now, using the instructional model we invented, the practice of linking mathematics and literature could benefit both fields: Literature study could help children engage in mathematics and mathematical study could help children both better understand literature and improve their own writing.

While the possible literary benefits of mathematics literary criticism and editing were being discussed by the study group, Doris, the fourth grade teacher, pushed the group to think deeply about Glenna Davis Sloan's book

The Child As Critic (1991), which describes children's literary criticism as a process that involves experiencing, responding to, reflecting on, and creating literature. By relating our work to existing practical and theoretical perspectives on children's literary criticism, a new synthesis emerged that combined, in an integrated and coordinated way, the perspectives of both mathematics education, and especially problem solving, and language arts instruction, particularly children's literary criticism and reader-response theory. This was exciting for we now succeeded both in inventing a new way of integrating the study of mathematics and literature during instruction and in providing that methodology with solid theoretical underpinnings.

In summary, the study group that formed to discuss children's mathematics trade books and to field test an assessment instrument went far beyond that initial purpose by engaging in mathematical literary criticism and editing as a form of problem solving that integrates mathematical and literary endeavors. The professional lives of the group members were enriched by their joint endeavors, and when they attempted to replicate with their students the experience they encountered in the study group, they invented a new instructional model.

In this book I will present that model. A concrete classroom example of mathematical literary criticism and editing will be described in Chapter 2. Its philosophical and pedagogical assumptions will be analyzed in Chapter 3. Then the tools necessary for using the model will be presented in Chapter 4, which focuses on the assessment of children's mathematics trade books, and Chapter 5, where the emphasis is on the mathematical enhancement of those books.

PERSPECTIVE ON THE MATHEMATICS
AND LITERATURE CONNECTION

The educational movement to integrate the teaching of mathematics and language arts is gaining in popularity among teachers. Heretofore it has been primarily a movement to use children's literature to facilitate the teaching of mathematics, but now numerous other directions are emerging, such as connecting mathematics with writing and combining mathematics and oral story telling. The remainder of this chapter will explore how this book fits into the context of that movement and then highlight some of the work that still lies ahead.

Reasons for Integrating Children's Books and Mathematics

Understanding why educators think it desirable to link mathematics and literature during instruction, and how this book relates to those reasons, allows its contributions to be set in a larger context. While many specific reasons exist, they can be grouped into the following seven general categories for ease of comprehension.

1. *To Help Children Learn Mathematical Concepts and Skills.* The professional literature on the mathematics and literature connection indicates that story books provide children with rich mathematics experiences and investigations, that can capture "the excitement and appeal of children's favorite stories to promote understanding of mathematics" (Hinton & Rafferty, 1990, p. 3) and "to develop concepts, solve problems and practice skills in a meaningful and interesting way" (Lovitt & Clarke, 1992, p. 237). This can mean many different things, including improving mathematics achievement test scores (Jennings, Jennings, Richey, & Dixon-Krauss, 1992), helping "children to experience the type of mathematics envisioned in the [NCTM] Standards while building on what grips the imagination of students and teachers—children's literature" (Welchman-Tischler, 1992, p. 1), or that mathematical "concepts can be greatly reinforced, enriched, and highlighted" (GEMS, 1993, p. 9).

The professional literature has hardly mentioned how connecting mathematics and literature can help children develop *literary* concepts and skills. One of the contributions of this book is that it demonstrates new ways in which linking mathematics and literature during instruction can help children simultaneously learn both mathematics and literary concepts and skills.

2. *To Provide Children With a Meaningful Context for Learning Mathematics.* Most educators' interest in mathematics story books centers on the ability of those books to provide children with a meaningful context for learning mathematics and seeing it function in their everyday world. For most writers this means that children's literature places mathematics in a familiar setting that children can identify with and which feels relevant and interesting to them. This setting can be one that relates to their current everyday world, to the real world they might face in the future, or to a fantasy world into which children can project themselves.

Writers have cited many benefits to placing mathematics in a meaningful story context. Braddon, Hall, & Taylor (1993), for example, feel that "the marriage of math with quality literature fosters the realization that math is all around us" (p. xiii). According to Whitin and Wilde (1992), "Children's literature helps to break down the artificial dichotomy that sometimes exists between *learning* mathematics and *living* mathematics" (pp. 2–5). Lovitt & Clarke (1992) believe that "the context of the story gives a framework for the exploration of mathematical ideas and the practice of skills" and "provides a cognitive framework with lots of 'cognitive hooks,' that allow many pieces of information to be linked together and their interrelationships explored and established" (pp. 238–239). Griffiths & Clyne (1991) feel that putting mathematics in a story context allows children to think at higher conceptual levels.

The literature has yet to seriously pursue whether there are corresponding literary benefits to linking mathematics and children's literature during instruction. Providing an affirmative answer to this question and introducing new contexts that can provide children with meaningful learning in both subjects is one of the contributions of this book.

3. *To Facilitate Children's Development and Use of Mathematical Language and Communication.* Many books describe how teachers use children's literature to help students develop their ability to communicate mathematically and to use language to help themselves and others construct mathematical meanings and develop common mathematical understandings by modeling mathematical "situations using oral, written, concrete, pictorial, graphical, and algebraic methods" (NCTM, 1989, p. 78). Griffiths and Clyne (1991), for example, note that "children learn mathematics through using language" and that "the combination of mathematics and literature, used in conjunction with opportunities for talk and discussion, allows children to grapple with mathematical concepts in a meaningful context" and in meaningful ways (p. 3).

This book will provide a far more comprehensive description than currently exists of how integrating mathematics and literature instruction can facilitate the development and use of mathematical language. It will also explore how the development of mathematical language can help children to better understand, appreciate, and create children's literature.

4. *To Help Children Learn Mathematical Problem Solving, Reasoning, and Thinking.* At the core of mathematical activity is the ability to think, reason, and problem solve like a mathematician. Thus it should be no surprise that one of the benefits of "linking mathematics with literature [is that] . . . it will help students . . . learn problem solving" (Kolakowski, 1992, n.p.), help students in "developing mathematical thinking" (Griffiths & Clyne, 1991, p. 6), and help students to learn to reason like a mathematician. Linking children's literature and mathematics both poses interesting problems for children to solve and develops the intellectual endeavor of problem solving.

This book will provide both a new interpretation and a rigorous analysis of how linking mathematics and literature can help children learn mathematical problem solving, as well as a new way of viewing problem solving from the perspectives of children's literary criticism and vice versa. It will also introduce the previously unasked question of "How can linking mathematics and children's literature help children problem solve, think, and reason like a member of the literary community?"

5. *To Provide Children with a Richer View of the Nature of Mathematics.* Linking mathematics and children's books has the potential to provide

children with a richer, more realistic, and broader view of the nature and scope of mathematics. To Whitin and Wilde (1992), for example, "children's literature demonstrates that mathematics develops out of human experience" (p. 6) and "restores the aesthetic dimension to mathematical learning" (p. 14). Griffiths and Clyne (1991) state that "tying mathematics to stories humanizes the activity and . . . can provide a link between the complexity of the world around us and the highly structured discipline of mathematics" (p. 5). Finally, according to Burns (1992b), "incorporating children's books into math instruction helps students experience the wonder possible in mathematical problem solving and helps them see a connection between mathematics and the imaginative ideas in books" (p. 1).

The effect of linking mathematics and literature on children's views of literature is an issue that has been largely unexplored. One of the contributions of this book will be to offer new examples of how linking the two during instruction can provide children with a richer view of the nature of both literary and mathematical endeavors.

6. *To Provide Children with Improved Attitudes Toward Mathematics.* Advocates of linking mathematics and children's literature during instruction believe that doing so will improve children's attitudes toward mathematics, will promote children's enjoyment of mathematics, "will help students gain confidence in their mathematics abilities" (Kolakowski, 1992, n.p.), and will "help students become mathematically powerful" (Stariano, 1994, p. v). What educators face, and attempt to overcome with children's literature, are negative attitudes toward mathematics. In general, the hope is that if children encounter mathematics in the context of children's literature, then their interest in the literary experience—as well as their perception of it as relevant and pleasurable—will be extended to and associated with the accompanying mathematical experience.

One of the contributions of this book to the professional literature is to explore how linking mathematics and children's literature can provide children with an improved sense of power both as budding mathematicians and literary agents.

7. *To Help Children Integrate Mathematics and Literature Study.* Curricular integration is at the core of the movement to link mathematics and literature. Educators approach the topic in one of two different ways.

Most educators who integrate mathematics and literature use children's literature as a springboard to introduce a mathematical investigation, rather than beginning a mathematical investigation by focusing directly on the mathematical topic being explored. In this case, children's books—one type of object—are being integrated into mathematics and there is no intention of integrating the subject areas of mathematics and children's literature. Most educators who write about the mathematics and children's literature connection see children's books as "objects" that are absorbed into mathematics pedagogy in order to facilitate the study of mathematics.

Another way of integrating mathematics and children's literature is to combine study of these two different school subjects in such a way that by focusing on a trade book children simultaneously learn about both the fields of mathematics and literature, as they simultaneously deal with both mathematical and literary issues (Griffiths & Clyne, 1991; Kliman, 1993; Lovitt & Clarke, 1992). Here children explore a story while focusing on its mathematics and its literary elements at the same time, in such a way that their increased understanding of its mathematics helps them better understand the story and its literary components, and vice versa. Almost no one presents instructional methods that indicate that they view the mathematics and children's literature connection in this way, as integrating two equal elements with benefits accruing to both.

Introducing an instructional model that supports the simultaneous mathematical and literary growth of children, and analyzing its pedagogical and philosophical underpinnings, will be one of this book's major contributions.

The Need for Educational Methods and Philosophy

In a decade when the mathematics–literature connection is quickly gaining popularity, serious attempts must be made to develop vital and powerful methods of using children's literature and mathematics together to enhance instruction. Serious attempts must also be made to clarify the pedagogical and philosophical assumptions underlying the instructional methods that are developed. The literature thus far published on "how to use children's books to help teach mathematics" has introduced numerous methods of linking mathematics and literature, although much of what this literature has described lacks the pedagogical inspiration and effectiveness that educators deserve. Of greater concern is that the philosophical underpinnings of many of the methodologies introduced seem nonexistent. It is as though the necessary philosophical dialogue is of little concern to most (although not all) of those publishing in this area.

If pedagogically vital and philosophically sound methods of using children's literature and mathematics together are not developed, we are likely to be left with no other option than to jump on a bandwagon and indiscriminately use children's books within the mathematics classroom. This will do little more for education than contribute to the formation of yet another educational fad that will be quick to appear, be criticized, and disappear. The mathematics and literature connection holds too much promise for enriching the teaching of mathematics and literature to be turned into an educational fad and quickly dismissed as a viable instructional tool.

An intent of this book is to introduce a pedagogically vital and effective method of using children's trade books to simultaneously teach mathematics and literature and to begin the serious philosophical dialogue about why we should integrate the teaching of these subjects. No claim is made that the method presented is either the best or better than any other. At this point in the development of methods to simultaneously teach mathematics and literature, the goal should be to find methods that produce powerful learning experiences for children rather than finding the best method. Similarly, at this point in the development of our philosophical beliefs about why and how to teach literature and mathematics together, it is probably more important to provide models for the type of philosophical dialogue that should be taking place than to provide the ultimate philosophical justifications.

The Need for Standards of Excellence and Excellent Books

Advocates of the mathematics and children's literature connection write as though children's literature is a collection of marvelous books that grip the imagination of students and teachers so strongly that merely using those books will guarantee children wonderful learning experiences—because of the power of the literature itself. Unfortunately, not all children's trade books are superb literature, a fact readily acknowledged in the field of children's literature, but almost never mentioned by those writing about linking mathematics and literature.

Experts in children's literature seem to believe that about 2% of the children's trade books published are excellent, whereas those who write about children's mathematics trade books judge about 40% to be excellent.[1] These differences raise serious questions about the standards of excellence for children's books used by those promoting the mathematics and children's literature connection. In addition, a literature search indicates that no rigorous or carefully conceived assessment standards exist for children's mathematics trade books.[2] Constructing a comprehensive set of standards and beginning the discussion about which children's mathematics trade books are excellent and why would greatly help those involved in linking mathematics and literature to raise their standards of excellence for children's books and become critical readers of children's literature. This is one of the intentions of this book.

Serious attempts must also be made to develop superb children's trade books that present mathematical ideas in inspiring ways, books that can support teachers' attempts to use children's literature and mathematics together to enhance both areas during instruction. Asking teachers to work miracles without the necessary tools is setting the stage for the eventual failure of a practice that is too important to prematurely fail. Hopefully a set of standards for excellent children's mathematics trade books, in coordination with demands from educators for more and better books that are based on a new understanding of how the integration of mathematics and literature during instruction can lead to more meaningful learning experiences for children, will help bring into existence a body of literature far more powerful than what we currently have. Helping to stimulate the creation of better children's mathematics trade books is another of this book's goals.

2

The Doorbell Rang:
A Classroom Example
of Mathematical Literary
Criticism and Editing

This chapter describes a practical classroom example of mathematical literary criticism and editing, one of many ways in which mathematics and children's literature can be used together during instruction to help children have wonderfully enriching mathematical experiences and delightfully uplifting literary experiences.

The process begins by providing children with a literary experience with a children's book that contains mathematics. After experiencing, responding to, and reflecting on their literary encounter, children focus their attention on the book's mathematics, analyzing the meaning of that mathematics and the adequacy of its presentation. The children construct or reconstruct their understanding of the mathematics, then edit—enhance, or rewrite—the book in an attempt to clarify for others (as well as themselves) the mathematical and literary meanings underlying its story. The editing can involve altering or enhancing the book's language, diagrams, equations, illustrations, or other graphic representations. Once the book is edited, children look back to see what occurred and what they learned during the process.

The following classroom example of mathematical literary criticism and editing describes in detail how the process might occur in a classroom. All of the activities, analyses, and questions are drawn from actual occurrences in second, third, fourth, and fifth grade classrooms, and from teacher workshops. In Chapter 3 the process will be analyzed to highlight and explain its philosophical and pedagogical underpinnings.

THE EXAMPLE

The example of mathematical literary criticism and editing presented in this chapter will describe how *The Doorbell Rang* (Hutchins, 1986) might be used with third or fourth graders. Figure 2.1 provides an overview of the timeline that should aid in following the events across 12 days and in reflecting back on the example.

The Doorbell Rang is a story about sharing cookies that takes place in a kitchen. The opening page shows "Ma" taking a baking tray of cookies out of the oven. The first page of the story with dialogue shows Ma putting a plate of twelve cookies on a kitchen table in front of two children, with the following exchange (Figure 2.2):

> "I've made some cookies for tea," said Ma.
> "Good," said Victoria and Sam. "We're starving."
> "Share them between yourselves," said Ma.
> "I made plenty."

The next two pages of *The Doorbell Rang* set the pattern for the remainder of the book. The children, still at the kitchen table, are about to pick up cookies off the plate when the doorbell rings. The illustration of the children and Ma in the kitchen spreads across two facing pages, with text on both:

> "That's six each," said Sam and Victoria.
> "They look as good as Grandma's," said Victoria.
> "They smell as good as Grandma's," said Sam.
> "No one makes cookies like Grandma," said Ma as the doorbell rang.

Tom and Hannah enter, and the cookies must now be shared among four children. Before they can eat the cookies, the doorbell rings again and two more children enter. The six children get ready to share the twelve cookies, but before they can the doorbell rings again and six more children enter the kitchen. Just as the twelve children are about to eat their cookies the doorbell rings again, and again, and again. No one wants to open the kitchen door, but they eventually do and in walks Grandma with an enormous tray of cookies for everyone.

Day One

On the first day the teacher begins by reading *The Doorbell Rang* to the whole class. A class discussion follows, during which the teacher guides the class to talk about and reflect upon a few of the following questions:

FIGURE 2.1 Overview of mathematical literary criticism and editing with *The Doorbell Rang*

Day	Teacher Activity	Children's Activity	Grouping	Problem-solving level*
1	• Read the book • Lead discussions	• Experience book as literature • Respond to experience • Search for mathematics	Whole class	Find
2	• Facilitate group work • Facilitate writing • Lead discussion	• Examine book for math, math errors, and quality of math presentation	Small group Individual Whole class	Find
3	• Read & review • Facilitate group work • Lead discussion • Facilitate writing • Respond to journals	• As editors, children examine the book's math and how it is presented, and make suggestions in journals about how to improve the book	Whole class Small group Individual	Find Understand Devise
4	• Stage dramatic productions of the book's story	• Act out the story and mathematical variations of it	Whole class Small group	Understand
5	• Facilitate group work • Lead discussion • Facilitate individual work • Respond to journals	• Read teacher's comments to previous day's writing • As editors, children examine the book's characterization, plot, and language, making suggestions for improvement • Plan enhancement to book, illustrate such, and describe in journals	Individual Small group Whole class	Find Understand Devise
6	• Facilitate children writing plans for enhancing book in journals and carrying out plans	• Read teacher comments on their writing, revise their plans for enhancing the book, and begin implementing plans	Individual	Devise Carry out
7 8 9	• Facilitate children's work, convene small groups to discuss progress	• Carry out plans to enhance and rewrite the book • Discuss progress with peers	Individual Small group	Carry out Look back
10 11 12	• Structure activities • Facilitate individual presentation of work and class discussions	• Display, discuss, and evaluate their book enhancements. • Read enhanced books to younger children & discuss • Write letters to book's author to describe the project	Whole class Small group Individual	Look back

Problem solving levels:

Find = find a problem to solve
Understand = understand the book's math and story, and their presentation

Devise = devise a plan for enhancing the book
Carry out = carry out the plan
Look back = look back and reflect on one's endeavors

How did the book make you feel (and why)?

What did the book remind you of in your own life?

What was important in the book (and why)?

Did you like the book (and why)?

If you were to tell a friend about the book, what are three things that would be most important for your friend to know (and why)?

If you could be any character in the book, who would you be (and why)?

Did you think you knew what was going to happen at the end of the book, before the last pages were read (and why)?

The teacher then asks the class to think about several additional questions from the above list while the book is read a second time. The class discussion following this second reading focuses on these additional questions.

The first two readings of *The Doorbell Rang* help the children experience, enjoy, and respond to the book—getting to know its story and characters and starting to imaginatively project themselves into the story—before the actual analysis of it begins.

The teacher prepares the class for a third reading of the book with two questions to think about as the book is read:

FIGURE 2.2 Page 1 of *The Doorbell Rang*

"I've made some cookies for tea," said Ma.

"Good," said Victoria and Sam. "We're starving."

"Share them between yourselves," said Ma.

"I made plenty."

Is there any mathematics in the book that relates to its story (if there is, what is it and where is it)?

Is there any mathematics in the book that does not relate to its story (if there is, what is it and where is it)?

After *The Doorbell Rang* is read a third time, the teacher leads a whole class discussion of these two questions. The children's comments are summarized on a chalkboard as they are offered, with similar comments grouped together. This summary can take the form of a simple list, a spider chart, or some other classificatory system that relates similar themes.

Among the things about the book's mathematics directly related to the story that the children might note are:

- The cookies on the baking pan are arranged in three rows of four cookies when they come out of the oven.
- When the cookies are removed from the baking tray and placed on a plate on the kitchen table, they are randomly piled on the plate.
- The cookies should be able to be counted.
- There should be the same number of cookies on the baking pan as in the plate.
- You can count the cookies on the baking tray more easily than on the plate.
- There are different ways of counting the cookies on the baking tray (individually, adding by rows, adding by columns, multiplying).
- If you share the cookies between two children, each gets six cookies.
- If you share the cookies between three children, each gets four.
- If six children each get two cookies, there are twelve cookies altogether.
- If three children each get four cookies, there are twelve cookies altogether.
- The book is about sharing and division and multiplication.
- Multiplication and division do and undo sharing.
- You can count the number of cookies on Grandma's tray.
- You can figure out how many cookies each child will get if you add Grandma's cookies to the others.

Among the things about the book's mathematics the children might note that are *not* directly related to the story are:

- In the illustrations you can count the number of: kitchen chairs, children, adults, plates on the hutch next to the table, plates on the table, and dirty footprints on the floor.

- In the illustrations you can calculate how many more or fewer: children than chairs there are, children than adults there are, and boys than girls there are.
- You can describe the geometric pattern on: the linoleum kitchen floor, the table cloth, and Ma's dress.

Day Two

On the second day the children work with *The Doorbell Rang* in small groups; each group has a copy of the book, and the children are asked to examine it from a mathematical perspective. By reading the book themselves in a setting where they can get close to it, they are able to do such things as count the number of cookies on each page. The small group setting allows more children to be involved in discussions in which they can express their own ideas and question others' thoughts. The teacher guides the children's work with the book by having them seek answers to the following types of questions:

What mathematics might be found on each page of the book?
How might mathematical problems found in the book be solved?
How is the book's mathematics related to other mathematics you know?
Does the book make any mathematical errors or mistakes?
Are there any places where the book's mathematics is confusing?
Where in the book could its mathematics be better presented? (How?)

Working within their small groups, each child keeps a written record of his or her answers to these questions. This written work becomes part of a dialogue journal that the teacher and child use as one (of several) means of communication.

Later on the second day, after all the children have examined *The Doorbell Rang*, the teacher leads a whole class discussion of children's answers to these questions. The teacher records the answers of the class on a chalkboard, grouping similar answers together, so that the class can see the result of their joint endeavors. This list will be referred to again in the future, so if the answers cannot be left on the chalkboard for several days, they should be transferred to some other presentation medium (such as large sheets of paper). The following types of mathematical questions, contributions, conversations, and clarifications have occurred during this discussion:

- There are 12 cookies on the baking tray, arranged in three rows of four each. You get 12 if you: count them one by one; count the number in each row and add repeatedly (4, 8, 12); count the number in each column and add repeatedly (3, 6, 9, 12); or multiply the number in each row by the number in each column. These ways of counting, repeated adding, and multiplying all give the same answer; they are different ways of doing the same thing. It is easier to find out how many cookies there are on the baking tray than on the plate because they are neatly arranged in rows and columns.

- Whoever illustrated the book could not count very well because on the second to last page of the book Grandma has 59 cookies on her tray (or is it 58?) while on the next page, after taking several steps into the kitchen, she has 68 cookies on her tray.

- The book's first page with text should say how many cookies there are on the tray, instead of just saying "I've made some cookies for tea" because if you are sitting far from the teacher while the book is read, the cookies are too small to count.

- The text on the book's first page could be confusing when Ma tells the children to "Share them [the cookies] between yourselves." Sharing does not have to mean "sharing equally." Many children with siblings are familiar with things not being "shared equally" with brothers or sisters. The book never says to "share so each person has the same number of cookies," even if that is what it means. A book should say what it means.

- At the end of the first page of text the book should ask "How many cookies will Victoria and Sam each get?" After all, this is what children want to know.

- There are different ways of figuring out how many cookies Victoria and Sam will each get if they share 12 cookies equally among themselves. One way is to divide the cookies between Victoria and Sam using the "one for you and one for me" method until you run out of cookies and each will then have 6. Another way is to guess and just put a bunch in one pile for Victoria (let's try 5) and then put the same number of cookies on another pile for Sam (that's another 5). Then see if there are any left (2 are still left), and share them equally between Victoria and Sam (1 cookie to each). Then both children will each have 6 cookies. (Children can be asked to demonstrate with manipulatives their interpretations of how the sharing process might take place.)

- The book could be improved if it had a small picture on some pages showing how the cookies were shared. Should it show the action of sharing or simply how many each person gets after the sharing is completed?

- Is the book about division or multiplication? Whenever you divide cookies up (as in $12 \div 2 = 6$) you also end up with a multiplication problem (as in $2 \times 6 = 12$). How are division and multiplication related?

- The author never writes down the mathematics equation for division. How do we write division? How do we say division? Is it, "12 divided by 2 is

6?" Is it, "2 goes into 12 is 6?" Is it, "12 goes into 2 is 6?" Is it, "12 divided by 2 equals 6?"

Day Three

On the third day, the teacher summarizes the whole-class discussion of the previous day while rereading the book to the class and pointing out the relevance of their comments to the book. The teacher then organizes small groups in which the children pretend that they are the editors of a publishing company that produces children's books containing mathematics. Their job is to locate mathematics in the book that is either incorrect or not easily visible and decide on what questions or suggestions might be made to the author to help her improve her book. While meeting in their small groups, the children are to discuss the following questions:

> Which parts of the book would you like the author and illustrator to change in order to clarify or correct the book's mathematics for the reader? Why is each part of the book that needs to be changed inadequate?
> How would you suggest that the author or illustrator improve each part of the book that was found to be mathematically inadequate? How would each suggestion improve the book?

After the small groups meet to discuss these questions, the teacher calls the class together to discuss their thoughts about both the inadequacies of the book and how the book might be improved. Some of the suggestions for improving the book that children have invented include:

- Make the cookies on the cookie plate more distinct.
- Make the plates on the hutch next to the kitchen table more distinct. Make sure that the number of plates on the hutch and the table remains constant throughout the book. (They vary.)
- Number the book's pages.
- "Ma" spends most of her time mopping the floor while children continue to enter the room. Find something better for her to do, such as getting out cups of milk or tea for the children to have with their cookies.
- Add a border to the page that: shows how the cookies are divided among the children, contains mathematics equations, asks the reader questions such as "How many cookies will each child have now?" or shows geometrical patterns such as those in Ma's dress.
- Put a plastic packet in the back of the book with pretend cookies and plates so that the reader can act out the story while it is being read.

- Put questions in the back of the book that describe things for children reading the book to look for. For example: "Describe the pattern in Ma's dress, on pages 4 and 5." "What is the sum of the number of plates on the hutch and the kitchen table, on pages 10 and 11?" "How many cookies will each child get to eat, if all of the cookies on the last page of the book are shared evenly?"
- Put a speaking bubble over the cat's head, a child's head, or in one of the puffs of steam from the tea kettle that has the division equation that says how many cookies each child will get.
- Have a flip up tab on every other page of the book that contains on it the question "How many cookies will each child get if they share the cookies equally?" Put the answer to the question under the flip up tab.
- Put a window in the room that has an illustration of how the cookies could be divided among the children. Maybe the illustrations could go on the stove door or in a thought bubble over the cat's head.
- Have only six chairs around the kitchen table. No family with only two children would have as many chairs around the kitchen table as there are in *The Doorbell Rang*. With only six chairs, when there are six or twelve children, we can ask "How many children will have to sit in each chair?"
- On the story's first page with text have Ma say "I've made a dozen cookies for tea" instead of "I've made some cookies for tea." Then have a speaking bubble over the cat's head that says "A dozen is the same as 12."
- On the bottom of the story's first page with text put the question "How many cookies will each child get?"
- Have the third sentence on the story's first page with text say "Share them equally between yourselves" instead of "Share them between yourselves."
- Have Ma say something that confirms that the children did the cookie division correctly.
- Put Grandma's recipe for chocolate chip cookies in the back of the book. Making cookies is fun, as well as requiring measurement.

One of the difficulties for the teacher will be to keep children focused on the mathematics topic desired—in this example, division. Children will want to focus on all other types of mathematical situations that arise within the book, such as keeping the number of plates on the hutch and kitchen table constant throughout the book. As long as children focus on at least the division story, they should be allowed to also pursue other avenues of mathematical investigation. Children will also want to focus on situations that are not mathematical, such as not letting the cat sit on the cookie plate or the need to put a flame in the stove's burner under the teapot. The children's exploration of topics other than division may be frustrating for the teacher, but part of posing an open-ended problem to children involves having the patience to let them pursue a variety of concerns, as long as they also remain cognizant of the mathematical issues that need to be considered.

Following the discussion of the book's inadequacies and the possible ways of improving it, each child is asked to write in their dialogue journal a brief description of what they think are the book's most significant mathematical inadequacies, why these are problems, which of them they might choose to rectify if they were to rewrite the book, and what their suggestions are for how to rectify each of the book's inadequacies. Prior to the next day, the teacher responds to those journals entries to help children focus on the book's mathematical problems they would like to try to rectify.

Day Four

On the fourth day of working with *The Doorbell Rang* the whole class enacts a dramatic production of the story. The teacher selects children to play different roles, and the children discuss how they might demonstrate the mathematics that needs to be done as each additional group of children enters Victoria's and Sam's kitchen and the cookies need to be shared in yet another way. Two roles are added to the dramatic production: a "mathematical commentator," who tells the audience what is occurring mathematically, and a "mathematical recorder," who records on the chalkboard the mathematics relevant to the different actions in the play as they take place. For example, when Victoria and Sam are joined in their kitchen by Tom and Hannah after the first ringing of the doorbell, the mathematical commentator might say, "There were 2 children in the kitchen, 2 more children joined them, and now there are 4 children in the kitchen." To accompany this, the mathematical recorder might write on the board "$2 + 2 = 4$." To describe the division that will accompany this situation, the mathematical commentator might say "12 cookies that are divided evenly among 4 children equals 3 cookies for each child" and the mathematical recorder might follow this by recording the equation on the chalkboard. The planning for the production of the play would involve much clarifying, amplifying, and extending of the book's mathematics, with demonstrations of how to physically act out, orally deliver, and symbolically record the story's mathematics. It must be stressed that this is an extremely important part of the process of helping the children understand the book's mathematics. Once the dramatic production is planned, it is performed for the class.

After the dramatic production is completed, the teacher describes how the story can be changed. One change might involve starting with Ma cooking 16 cookies and Victoria and Sam being joined, first by 2 more children, then 4 more children, and then by 8 more children. The children are asked how this might be acted out with manipulatives if they used chips (poker chips, bingo chips, etc.) to represent cookies, a medium sized paper plate to represent a serving platter, and small paper plates to represent the different children. Critical here would be the processes of demonstrating how to physically divide the 16 cookies among the increasingly large number of children, to use oral language to describe the action, and to use symbolic writing to record the verbalizations.

The teacher then organizes the class into small groups of four children each. The small groups read and enact three variations of *The Doorbell Rang* story, variations that the teacher writes for the class. The children in each group take turns in the roles of reader of the story, manipulator of chips and paper plates, mathematical commentator, and mathematical recorder. The three stories involve 8 cookies and the sequence of 2, 4, and 8 children; 20 cookies and the sequence of 2, 4, 5, 10, and 20 children; and 24 cookies and the sequence of 2, 3, 4, 6, 12, and 24 children.

Day Five

On the fifth day the teacher summarizes the dramatizations of the previous day. The teacher then tells the children that they will meet in small groups and pretend that they once again are the editors of a publishing company that produces children's mathematics books. This time they are to decide where the book's story, characterization, and language are weak and what questions or suggestions might be made to the book's author to help her improve her book so that it will provide readers with a richer mathematical and literary experience. The teacher presents a brief description of what a plot is and discusses with the class what it means for a book's plot to be well-developed and imaginative in such a way that it flows logically, believably, and sensibly from one idea to the next. This is followed by a discussion of how a book's characters are depicted, as well as what it means for a book's characters to be well portrayed and believable. Finally, how a book's language contributes to the development of its story and characterization is explored. While meeting in their small groups, the children are to discuss the following:

> If you were an editor, which parts of the book might you like the author to change in order to improve the book's story, characters, or language?
> Why is each part of the book that needs to be changed inadequate?
> How might the author improve each inadequate part of the book?
> How would each suggested change improve the book?

Strategies that children can use to explore these questions include acting out parts of the book's story to test out new roles for characters, brainstorming about alternate language for the story, and using logical reasoning to test for such things as completeness and consistency within the book's existing plot and characterization.

After the small groups meet to discuss these questions, the teacher calls the class together to discuss their thoughts. Some suggestions for improving the book that children have invented include:

- Why is Ma constantly mopping the floor while the kids still have on their dirty shoes. Why can't Ma do something more believable. My Mom would do something like get glasses out of the cupboard and serve the kids milk. We could then count, add, and subtract the glasses. (*A comment on characterization.*)
- I don't like Ma's comment to the kids on page 19 that maybe they should quickly eat their cookies before opening the door [made when the doorbell starts ringing for the fourth time, after the twelve cookies had been distributed to the twelve children now in the kitchen]. Nobody's mother would say that. A mother might say, "What should we do?" My Ma would never tell me to eat up the cookies before I opened the door to let my friends in the kitchen. (*A comment on characterization.*)
- The story begins with Ma saying "I've made some cookies for tea." My Ma never gives me tea. She might give me milk, soda, or hot chocolate. And what happens with the drink. It never shows up for the rest of the story. Why can't Ma be pouring the drink instead of mopping the floor. That's what my Ma would do. (*A comment on plot.*)
- On the first page of the story Ma says, "I've made some cookies for tea." Wouldn't it be better if she said, "I've made 12 cookies for tea" or "I've made a dozen cookies for tea"? Both "12" and "dozen" are better than "some." Which would be the best word to use? (*A comment on language.*)
- At the end of the first page of the story Ma should ask the kids how many cookies they will each get. Then the first sentence on the next page follows naturally. (It begins, "That's six each.") Ma might say, "How many cookies will each of you get?" or "How many will each of you get to eat?" Which would be the best sentence? And where should it be placed? Should it go at the end of the last sentence or on a new line by itself? (*A comment on language.*)

These types of literary suggestions will give the class much to think about and to discuss, for they have no simple answers. The teacher's task will be to clarify the literary issues raised by the class, ask how they pertain to enhancing the book, help the class offer a variety of solutions to the book's perceived inadequacies, and make sure that no closure is reached about what might be changed or how it might be changed. Determining the book's literary inadequacies and how it might be improved are serious literary endeavors that each child should have a chance to personally struggle with and resolve.

Later on the fifth day the teacher hands back the students' dialogue journals so the children can read the teacher's comments. Then with the benefit of the teacher's comments, their classmates' comments on rectifying the book's mathematical inadequacies (from the class discussion on Day Three), new insights into the operation of division (from the dramatizations of Day Four), and the discussion of the book's literary components (earlier on Day Five), the children begin the process of planning how they will rewrite or re-illustrate *The Doorbell Rang*. In their dialogue journals they write a brief plan for how they will change the book, and they illustrate the changes by putting self-stick note tabs that describe or illustrate each desired change in the book on a copy of *The Doorbell Rang* that is given to them for this purpose. (The note tabs will later be removed from the books when the final editing process takes place.) At the end of the day the teacher examines the children's dialogue journals and "note tabbed" books and writes comments in the journals about the plans for rewriting.

Day Six

On day six the children read the teacher's comments in their journal and then begin carrying out their plan for rewriting *The Doorbell Rang*. The material used during the rewriting can vary, based upon the teacher's intention for the class and the children's abilities. A few of the beginning points from which the rewriting can proceed are as follows:

Children can be given only paper and colored markers. If they begin with these few materials, a great deal of changing of the original illustrations and rewriting of the book's text is likely to take place.

Children can be given copies of the book to rewrite. Inexpensive versions of many children's books are available through school-oriented publishing houses, such as Scholastic. Students can paste paper over words or illustrations they want to change and write on the paper. They can also write and draw directly in their books. If books need to be reused, children can write and draw on self-stick note tabs, which can be removed without damage to a book when the activity is completed.

Children can be given photocopies of the book to rewrite. Some publishers will grant permission to make a limited number of photocopies of a book for a small fee. Some types of photocopying allow the ink to be erased, so that text can be easily removed or changed. Illustrations, equations, diagrams, and so forth can be drawn into the book where desired.

The goal of the editing, rewriting, and re-illustrating process is not to reinvent the story of the book or to fully illustrate the book from scratch, but rather to show how the original can be improved by enriching its mathematical and literary components. The range of changes that might be pursued by children include:

- Changing the book's text. For example, if the first line of text in the book was changed from "I've made some cookies for tea" to "I've made 12 cookies for snack."
- Adding text to the book. For example, if at the end of the first page of the text the following sentence were added: "'How many cookies will you each get?' asked Ma."
- Adding equations to the book. For example, if on each page where division takes place, a division equation describing the action were tactfully presented.
- Adding diagrams to the book. For example, by adding diagrams to appropriate pages to show how the division that occurs in the story might be accomplished.
- Adding manipulatives to the book. For example, add poker chips (to represent cookies) and small paper plates (to represent children), along with instructions on how to use them in coordination with the story's events, so that readers can act out the book's mathematics while it is read.
- Correcting the book's errors. For example, by making the number of cookies on Grandma's tray on the book's last two pages the same.
- Altering the book's illustrations. For example, by if the cookies were arranged on the serving platter in a way that portrayed a mathematical structure.

Days Seven Through Nine

During the next several days children carry out their plans for rewriting *The Doorbell Rang.* As this takes place, the teacher communicates with children through their journals about their rewriting endeavors, has individual conferences with children to discuss their efforts and help them clarify their ideas, and assembles small groups of children to discuss their work. These discussions—whether in journal, conference, or small group format—allow children to express and clarify their ideas, thoughtfully listen to others, and respond to each other's endeavors.

Days Ten Through Twelve

When children have completed their editing, their rewritten books are put on display, along with the original, for everyone in the class to examine.

Later, the teacher will have each child present his or her book to the class and do such things as compare it to the original, explain what was changed, give the reasons for making the changes, and evaluate the effectiveness of the endeavors.

Two additional activities aid the process of looking back and reflecting on what has been accomplished. One involves having each child reading the original book and his or her edited book to a first or second grader to see how the younger child understands and reacts to each. Reading the two books to a test audience and observing responses allows the children to reflect on the effectiveness of their alterations and serves as a way to review their endeavors. The children who rewrote *The Doorbell Rang* will also be listening to younger children's conceptions and misconceptions about division. With guidance from the teacher during class discussions, the younger children's conceptions and misconceptions of division will help the older children both reflect on what they have learned and put their new understanding of mathematics in perspective.

The second activity involves having children write letters—book reviews—to the author or publisher of *The Doorbell Rang* describing what they consider to be the strengths and weaknesses of the book, supported by their reasoning. This activity provides an opportunity for children to reflect on the entire *The Doorbell Rang* project and their endeavors in mathematical literary criticism and editing, but more importantly it empowers the budding mathematical problem solvers and literary critics to use their skills to make a difference in the larger world beyond the confines of the school.

VARIATIONS

The Doorbell Rang example of mathematical literary criticism and editing lasted twelve days. Many variations on the example exist. Some teachers combine their mathematics, reading, and language arts periods to complete the project in one week. Some teachers feel more secure using structured worksheets—where questions were asked and spaces left for children to respond—rather than unstructured dialogue journals. Mathematical literary criticism and editing can involve individuals each enhancing a book, small groups working on books together, or a whole class working together on a single book. One class, where children were organized into small groups, enhanced a single copy of *The Doorbell Rang* by having each group take responsibility for implementing the class enhancement plans for a single two-page spread. The activity of displaying the enhanced books can involve a variety of audiences, from younger children to older children, from parents to librarians. One teacher who has tried mathematical literary criticism and editing with her classes for several years, has her current fourth graders show their books to her fifth grade graduates. I occasionally receive letters from children that describe their endeavors.

Mathematical literary criticism and editing can be used to introduce new concepts and to review concepts already supposedly learned, to help children both to construct new mathematical meanings and to clarify or enrich current meanings. Usually second and third graders focus on constructing an understanding of division while fourth and fifth graders focus on reviewing, clarifying, and reconstructing their understanding of division. In addition, the mathematical meanings constructed by children as they work with *The Doorbell Rang* do not have to be limited to division. One second-grade teacher used the book to review addition and subtraction while at the same time introducing division. A fifth-grade teacher used the book to review division while focusing on fractions.

Mathematical literary criticism and editing can be used with many books. Some favorites are *Alexander, Who Used to Be Rich Last Sunday* (Viorst, 1978), *The Philharmonic Gets Dressed* (Kuskin, 1982), *The King's Chessboard* (Birch, 1988), *Inch by Inch* (Lionni, 1960), and *Caps For Sale* (Slobodkina, 1940/1987).

Mathematical literary criticism and editing is an exciting activity for both pre-service and in-service teachers. It gives them a new perspective on children's literature, its uses during instruction, and their power to affect their world as mathematicians and literary critics. Teachers can engage in mathematical literary criticism and editing as part of short in-service workshops held in schools, as part of graduate and undergraduate pre-service and in-service mathematics education courses, and as part of research seminars on the teaching of mathematics and literacy.

Teachers have engaged in numerous interesting projects. One teacher enhanced *The Doorbell Rang* to use with her first grade class to help them learn addition, subtraction, and geometric patterns. Addition and subtraction were dealt with by having Ma serve the children milk using twelve mugs that were prominently placed on a shelf over the sink at the beginning of the story. (Addition and subtraction related to how many cups remained on the shelf or were in use at any time.) Geometric patterns were introduced by creating page extenders that highlighted some of the many patterns in the story: in the children's and Ma's clothes, in the tablecloth, and in the rug. Another teacher enhanced *The Doorbell Rang* by changing the names of the book's characters to those of the children in her second grade class.

One group of teachers had a lengthy discussion about the cultural setting of *The Doorbell Rang*. They enhanced the book in ways that reflected the setting in which they worked: inner city schools, suburban schools, schools with diverse populations, schools with specific homogenous populations, etc.

Some of their concerns related to the following issues: What should be the names and races of the story's children so that they reflected the cultures of their students? What types of clothes and toys should the story's children have so that they mirror those of their students? What types of food and beverages should be served in the story (serving "cookies and tea" says something about one's culture in comparison to serving "cookies and milk" or "cookies and coke")? What activities should Ma engage in that would reflect the activities that their students' mothers might engage in (for example, does Ma bake or purchase cookies)? What is the correspondence between the decoration of the kitchen in the story and in their students' homes (for example, how many children have rugs under their kitchen tables)?

Perhaps the most striking thing about teachers' enhancements of *The Doorbell Rang* has been the wide range of devices they created to enrich the story: page extenders with illustrations on them; stove doors that opened that had mathematics problems on the outside and answers on the inside; laminated pages on which children could write answers to questions asked in the text; tea cups made out of vinyl reusable "stickees" that could be moved about and temporarily affixed to laminated pages of the book; question-and-answer wheels that presented questions and then displayed answers when children pulled a tab; and treasure hunts where children have to search for certain specified mathematical relationships on the pages of the book. (These are described in Chapter 5.) Teachers inspired each other with their creations and enhanced their feelings about themselves as powerful mathematical and literary agents. Many left their encounter with mathematical literary criticism and editing asking important questions about their role as teachers when using children's books with children, as well as with questions about extending the model to other areas of the school curriculum.

Having presented a practical classroom example of mathematical literary criticism and editing in this chapter, we now turn our attention to uncovering and clarifying the pedagogical and philosophical assumptions underlying the model in Chapter 3.

3

The Doorbell Kept Ringing!
A Pedagogical Model
Proposed and Analyzed

Mathematical literary criticism and editing, as embodied in the example presented in the previous chapter, can be examined from numerous perspectives in order to clarify its pedagogical and philosophical assumptions. This chapter will examine the endeavor from the perspectives of problem solving, literary criticism, and the power and function of language.

PROBLEM SOLVING

Most educators believe that at the core of mathematical activity is the ability to solve problems, think, and reason like a mathematician. Exactly what is meant by that, however, can vary a great deal. Some educators view these endeavors as open-ended activities in which children both pose the problems to be solved and seek unique, idiosyncratic solutions to those problems; some view them as structured activities that involve applying one of several problem-solving strategies; some view them as modeling mathematical activities with physical manipulatives; and some view them as comprehension and calculation activities during which children fill in worksheets.

The goals underlying mathematical literary criticism and editing are to help children learn a specific approach to problem solving, to provide them with a rich and meaningful problem-solving experience, and to create an instructional environment that is itself defined by a particular approach to problem solving. The approach is an enhanced version of Polya's four-phase problem-solving method that emphasizes open-ended problem solving. The enhanced version of Polya's problem-solving method, the type of problem used in this instructional model, and the nature of the instructional environment underlying mathematical literary criticism and editing will be discussed in this order.

Polya's Problem-Solving Scheme Enhanced

One of the major models for mathematical problem solving is Polya's (1957) four-phase method, which involves (1) understanding the problem to be solved, (2) devising a plan to solve the problem, (3) carrying out the plan, and (4) looking back to see the effectiveness of the plan. Polya's method does not offer a prescribed set of strategies for solving problems or an algorithm for obtaining solutions to problems; rather, it is a general method for approaching problems in a systematic manner.

In mathematical literary criticism and editing, Polya's four phases are expanded to five. The additional phase of "finding a problem," the first in which children engage, involves *having the child discover a problem that the child feels needs to be solved.* This includes having the child find or invent a problem that exists in the child's world, notice that it is a problem worthy of being solved, and personally engage the problem.

This enhanced model provides the major design element for the instructional environment in which children learn. However, the model is not directly taught to children; they do not learn an algorithm that they are then expected to apply deliberately and directly to problems (or problem-solving situations) that they encounter in their lives. Rather, the enhanced model provides the logic that defines the nature of the problem-solving environment within which children learn—both in terms of the nature of the activities engaged in by children and their sequence. It is assumed that children will learn the problem-solving approach that is modeled for them by the environment in which they learn.

If Polya's enhanced model were to be "taught" to children, they would be told about it only after they had engaged in mathematical literary criticism and editing, which itself provides an exemplar for that approach to problem solving. It would be presented to them as a way of "looking back" over what had been accomplished during the process of mathematical literary criticism and editing. This "looking back" process would provide children with an "advance organizer" designed to guide their future problem solving.

Each of the phases of the enhanced model will now be examined.

Find a Problem. During mathematics instruction teachers usually give children well-defined problems to solve, problems whose solutions involve discovering single well-defined answers. In contrast, mathematical literary criticism and editing asks children themselves to find the mathematical problems they will solve, to define the nature of those problems and their solutions, and to become personally involved in solving them. Finding their own problems to solve is important for children (Brown & Walters, 1983).

In *The Doorbell Rang* example, children begin the process of "finding a problem" on the first day when they examine the story to see if it contains mathematics. The process continues on the second day as children explore the book's mathematical and presentational inadequacies. During the third day children are asked to reexamine the book—in light of the inadequacies discovered by the individuals, small groups, and class as a whole the previous day—as they begin to define the problem with the book's inadequate mathematical presentation. On the fifth day the book's literary dimensions are explored to see how they contribute to the inadequate presentation of the story and mathematics. Children then continue to define the book's problem that they intend to solve by writing about it in their dialogue journal. The teacher, in turn, responds to each child's writing, either encouraging their engagement with the problems chosen or guiding them to the book's inadequacies that they are capable of improving.

The process of "finding a problem" with the book that needs resolution, exploring the nature of the problem, confirming that it really is a problem, and personally engaging the problem is an important process that can take several days to complete. It both helps define the nature of the instructional environment and constitutes the first step in the problem-solving process that children learn.

Understand the Problem. For Polya (1957), understanding a problem involves being able to "repeat the statement" of the problem, "state the problem fluently," and "point out the principal parts of the problem, the unknown, the data, the conditions" (pp. 6–7). In mathematical literary criticism and editing, understanding the problem involves both understanding a book's mathematical and literary shortcomings, and understanding its mathematics.

A book's mathematical shortcomings cannot be fully understood, nor can a plan for compensating for the mathematical inadequacies of a book be formulated, until the mathematics to be corrected or clarified in the book is understood by the child. As Polya (1957) says about devising a plan, "it is hard to have a good idea if we have little knowledge of the subject, and impossible to have it if we have no knowledge. Good ideas are based on past experience and formerly acquired knowledge" (p. 9).

Helping children understand a book's mathematics is central to mathematical literary criticism and editing. To accomplish this, the mathematics is not simply presented to children in abstract symbolic form, but rather in the context of the book's story so that they both experience it and learn to re-present it in their own words. Re-presenting the book's mathematics helps children learn it and clarify their understanding of it. Such re-presenting raises to a conscious, verbal, and symbolic level mathematics that children may only intuitively (and perhaps partially or incorrectly) understand. Doing so also allows the teacher or other children to assess a child's understandings for possible errors. If errors in understanding exist, they can be corrected before the child proceeds to edit the book. Taking time to make sure that children understand a story's mathematics is a critical part of mathematical literary criticism and editing, for it would be foolish to let a child rewrite, reillustrate, or re-present a book's mathematics if the child did not understand that mathematics to begin with.

In *The Doorbell Rang* example, the process of "understanding the problem" that relates to understanding a book's mathematical and literary shortcomings is first undertaken during the second day, when the children explore the book's mathematical inadequacies. It is later explored when the children do such things as examine the way in which the book's literary elements enhance or detract from its presentation of its mathematics.

Understanding the problem, as it relates to understanding the mathematics in *The Doorbell Rang*, is highlighted on the fourth day with the story's dramatization, in which the book's mathematics is presented with physical manipulatives and is carefully explained in connection with the children's actions, verbalizations, and writing. The mathematics is presented in this manner because it is assumed that the children are in the concrete operational stage of development. Children are therefore asked to understand the mathematics in ways that are consistent with their abilities: by concretely acting—or operating—on a physical representation of the division problems in the book. After the whole-class dramatization, children are asked to imitate the mathematical processes learned by working in small groups in which they re-enact variations of the story by taking on the roles of reader of the story, manipulator of chips and paper plates, mathematical commentator, and mathematical recorder. In doing so the children are re-presenting their mathematical meanings to each other and assessing each other's mathematical meanings so that any lack of understanding can be rectified as they learn to physically demonstrate, describe, record, and assess mathematical meanings.

At one level, the mathematical environment in which children learn is now defined by the activity of understanding the book's mathematics. At another level, children are now learning that understanding the book's mathematics will help them better understand its inadequacies and ways of rectifying those inadequacies.

Devise a Plan.   In order to systematically proceed to mathematically enhance a book, a plan must be devised that indicates which of its inadequacies will be rectified and how such will be accomplished. A number of educators have developed strategies to facilitate mathematical problem solving at this stage (strategies that are also frequently useful at other stages of problem solving). Polya (1957) offers suggestions such as "draw a figure," "introduce suitable notation," and examine "a related problem" (pp. 7–9). Other educators offer such strategies as write an equation, draw a picture, construct a table, act out the problem, look for a pattern, relate a new problem to familiar problems, work backwards, use logical reasoning, guess and check, make a model, and brainstorm. The categories of problem-solving strategies presented by Baroody (1993), Burns (1992a), and Hoogeboom and Goodnow (1987) are presented in Figure 3.1, with similar strategies next to each other across the columns.

All of these strategies are suitable for use in devising a plan to mathematically enhance a book during mathematical literary criticism and editing. What needs to be done is to slightly rephrase the strategies so that at one level they designate how to clarify the meaning of a book's mathematics and its story while at another level they facilitate thought about ways of enhancing a book's mathematical and literary elements. *The Doorbell Rang*

FIGURE 3.1 Selected popular problem-solving strategies

Polya	Baroody	Burns	Hoogeboom & Goodnow
introduce suitable notation	write an equation	write an equation	
		use objects	act out or use objects
	act out the problem, make a model, draw a picture, or draw a diagram	act it out	
		make a model	
draw a figure		draw a picture	make a picture or diagram
	organize the data in a list, table, or chart and look for patterns	construct a table	use or make a table
		make an organized list	make an organized list
	look for a pattern by examining specific examples	look for a pattern	use or look for a pattern
	use logical reasoning		use logical reasoning
	work backwards	work backward	work backwards
	simplify a problem and look for patterns	solve a simpler (or similar) problem	make it simpler
examine a related problem	relate a new problem to familiar problems		
	guess and check	guess and check	guess and check
			brainstorm

example contained the following strategies for clarifying its mathematics: adding manipulatives to the book so children can act out the story's mathematics; adding diagrams to show the meaning of the story's mathematics; and adding equations to describe the book's mathematics. Strategies that could help children think about ways of enhancing literary dimensions of *The Doorbell Rang* include acting out the book's story to test out new roles for characters, brainstorming about alternative language for the story, and using logical reasoning to plan alternative plots. Note that these "problem-solving strategies" are never directly "taught" to children during mathematical literary criticism and editing, although they are often modeled for children and children often use them.

Devising a plan for mathematically enhancing a children's book is one of the major activities that defines the instructional environment in which mathematical literary criticism and editing takes place. Children also learn that one of the steps in solving problems is devising a plan. In *The Doorbell Rang* example, children begin to work on devising a plan on the second day. On the fifth day they describe their plan in their dialogue journals. This gives the children a chance to think through their plans before actually beginning to enhance the book. It also gives the teacher a chance to respond to their plans by encouraging the children's endeavors as well as making sure that they do not pursue unproductive, incorrect, or overly ambitious endeavors.

Carry Out the Plan. To conceive a plan and to carry it out are two different things. In devising a plan, a child must imagine a transformed book. In carrying out a plan, a child must actually transform a book. Devising a plan requires that the child engage in one type of creativity: inventing alternatives that more clearly, effectively, and accurately present the book's mathematics and story. Carrying out a plan requires that the child engage in another type of creativity: working through the details of actually rewriting text, constructing tables and charts, drawing illustrations, and making sure the edited parts of the book fit together in a pleasing way that enhance the book's story. While carrying out the plan, children should monitor their endeavors in order to determine whether their plan is having the desired effect, whether a new point of view or perspective on the problem is needed, whether all the pertinent information is effectively presented, whether errors or inconsistencies in presentation occur, and whether an easier or more elegant way of accomplishing one's goals might be discovered. Evaluating one's success while implementing and revising a plan is an important part of successfully carrying it out.

In *The Doorbell Rang* example, children spent the sixth through ninth days enhancing the book. Seven different ways of enhancing the book are described, including altering text, adding diagrams, and adding mathematical equations. Executing them is similar to the process of carrying out problem-solving strategies that result in the solution of a problem. When carrying out their plans for improving a book, children should be given sufficient time to actually do the necessary editing. It is important that children not be asked to re-create a book entirely from scratch, for the goal is to rethink the presentation of the book's story and mathematics, not to spend hours attempting to reinvent the story or redraw professionally drawn illustrations.

Look Back. Once children have enhanced a book it is important for them to look back and see what they have accomplished. Polya (1957) describes this "looking back" phase of his problem-solving method thus:

> *Looking Back.* Even fairly good students, when they have obtained the solution of the problem and written down neatly the argument, shut their books and look for something else. By looking back at the completed solution, by reconsidering and reexamining the result and the path that led to it, they could consolidate their knowledge and develop their ability to solve problems. (pp. 14–15)

During mathematical literary criticism and editing, children need to look back at their endeavors to see the effectiveness of their plan, to examine the relationship of their edited book to the original, to reflect on the mathematics they have learned and clarified, to reflect upon the mathematical literary criticism and editing process in which they have engaged, to see the relationships of their endeavors to other real-world situations they might encounter, and to reflect on the problem-solving process they have used. If children simply put aside their work upon completing it, they are likely to miss many of the benefits of their endeavors. Reflecting upon what has been accomplished often provides a sense of perspective, greater understanding, and a set of advance organizers that can be used when similar problems are faced in the future.

"Looking back" is one of the major activities that defines the instructional environment in which mathematical literary criticism and editing takes place. It is also a critical stage in the problem-solving process. In *The Doorbell Rang* example, the process of looking back involves at least three activities.

In one activity children look back at their work by showing their enhanced book to the class, comparing it with the original, explaining what they changed, giving their reasons for these changes, and evaluating the effectiveness of their endeavors.

The second activity involves having the children read their mathematically enhanced books to younger children and then discuss their observations. In doing so, they compare younger children's responses to their book and the original version, explore younger children's understandings of and misunderstandings about division, and reflect on what they have recently learned about division.

The third activity involves having children review the entire *The Doorbell Rang* project, both so that they can reflect on the five-phase problem-solving process in which they engaged and so that they can write a letter describing their endeavors. Reflecting on the five-phase problem-solving process gives children a cognitive organizer to aid them in their future encounters with problems. Writing a letter empowers budding mathematical problem solvers and literary critics to use their new knowledge to make a difference in their larger world, beyond the confines of the school.

Open-Ended Versus Closed-Ended Problems

The problem posed by mathematical literary criticism and editing is how to analyze and enhance a children's mathematics trade book in order to provide its future readers with a richer and more wonderful mathematical and literary experience than the original book. As illustrated in *The Doorbell Rang* example, doing so involves multiple interconnected endeavors, such as understanding the book's story and mathematics; locating the story's essential and tangential mathematics; determining how literary elements such as theme, characterization, and language contribute to or detract from the story; determining the effectiveness of the book's presentation of its story and mathematics; determining alternative ways that the book's mathematics and literary elements can be clarified and presented, and projecting the impact of alternative presentations; deciding which way of mathematically enhancing the book complements and enriches its story the most; actually enhancing the book and evaluating the effect of those enhancements; and looking back on and reporting to others the significance of one's endeavors.

This type of problem is not frequently encountered by children in school. It is sometimes called an open-ended problem. In contrast, the problems usually found in textbooks are called closed-ended problems. Two popular types of closed-ended problems are exercises (for example, "22 × 33 = ?") and word problems (for example, "Mary has 4 cookies. She eats 2 cookies. How many does she have left?").

Comparing mathematical literary criticism and editing with traditional mathematical exercises and word problems highlights significant differences between these two types of problems—and the corresponding types of endeavors in which children engage—as the following brief discussion shows. Figure 3.2 summarizes these differences.

Answer. Mathematical exercises and word problems usually have a single correct answer; mathematical literary criticism and editing does not. It

FIGURE 3.2 Comparison of mathematical literary criticism (open-ended problems) and traditional exercises and word problems (closed-ended problems)

ATTRIBUTE	MATH LITERARY CRITICISM & EDITING: OPEN-ENDED PROBLEMS	EXERCISES & WORD PROBLEMS: CLOSED-ENDED PROBLEMS
Answer	Have more than one correct answer and encourage the invention of previously unimagined solutions	Have a single correct answer
Knowledge	Encourage the search for mathematical meanings and understanding	Give practice in applying an operation or algorithm recently learned
Focus	Focus on higher level thought processes	Involve a simple translation of words into an equation, graph, or table from which an answer can be extracted
Creativity	Encourage and value using a diverse range of problem-solving strategies	A limited number of acceptable solutions are assumed to exist
Time	Recognize the need for an extended time period to solve certain types of problems	Require a limited amount of time to solve
Range	Their solution is often facilitated by the coordinated use of a variety of diverse understandings and skills	Require a narrow range of mathematical endeavors to solve
Origin	Are discovered by children out of their own need to thrive in the situation in which they find themselves, and are pursued as their own problems	Are usually given to the child by a teacher, textbook, or other authoritarian source
Relevance	Are situationally and temporally relevant to children as problems they might encounter either during their everyday endeavors or within their fantasy life	Usually do not relate to either children's real worlds or their imaginary ones
Involvement	Entice children to become personally involved with them because they stimulate their imagination and sense of power	Usually do not entice the child to become personally involved with or immersed in them

involves analyzing, critiquing, and understanding a story and its mathematics and then finding more effective ways of re-presenting them. There is no one answer to this type of endeavor, and inventiveness in devising penetrating analyses and previously unimagined ways of enhancing a book are rewarded.

Knowledge. Mathematical exercises and word problems usually emphasize the practice and application of "skills." Mathematical literary criticism and editing helps children clarify and reconstruct their own and a book's meanings, primarily emphasizing "understandings" and "meanings" and secondarily emphasizing "skills." In *The Doorbell Rang* example, the primary emphasis is on understanding division, and calculating the answers to problems is a secondary by-product of understanding.

Focus. Closed-ended problems usually involve locating relevant information in a problem, calculations, or a simple translations of words into an equation, graph, or table from which an answer can be extracted. Mathematical literary criticism and editing involves higher-level thought processes, such as understanding, analyzing, reflecting, creating, and decision making, as they relate to the effectiveness of the presentation of a book's mathematics and story.

Creativity. Closed-ended problems are usually assumed to have a limited number of solutions and solution methods. Mathematical literary criticism and editing is assumed to have multiple solution methods. Problem solvers are encouraged to use a diverse range of strategies, and previously undiscovered solutions are highly valued. Creativity in seeing *The Doorbell Rang* from a new perspective or inventing new ways of enhancing its mathematical or literary meanings is rewarded.

Time. Mathematical exercises and word problems can usually be solved quickly. Open-ended problems frequently require an extended period of time for solution. For example, *The Doorbell Rang* example took 12 days to complete.

Range. Usually a narrow range of mathematical skills are needed to solve closed-ended problems, while mathematical literary criticism and editing requires the coordinated use of a wide range of diverse endeavors. For example, during the first several days of *The Doorbell Rang* example, the book's mathematics was located, the meaning of division was clarified, its mathematical and literary presentations were assessed, and decisions were made about which of its inadequacies would be rectified.

Origin. Mathematical exercises and word problems are usually given to children by a teacher, textbook, or other authoritarian source, and they are usually solved in order to meet requirements imposed on the child by others. In mathematical literary criticism and editing, children are given a book to analyze and enhance, but they themselves must identify the book's inadequacies (its "problems"), make them their own problems, invent their own ways of solving them (by enhancing the book), and enhance the book to their own satisfaction. In other words, children must themselves find the problems they will solve and solve them to their own satisfaction.

Relevance. Most mathematical exercises and word problems do not relate to either children's real everyday world or their fantasy world. Although they might be relevant to children in their everyday life if they occurred in their everyday life, they are irrelevant to them when they occur in a classroom or homework assignment. They are irrelevant because the situational and temporal context in which they arise makes them irrelevant—the context of being given on a sheet of paper with numerous other problems, each of which is usually about something different, in a very condensed symbolic verbiage, outside of the context of any rich story into which children can project themselves. Such problems are not located in a context that is rich enough in its dramatic elements—such as character development, plot, surprise, conflict, and suspense—that the child is drawn into the context in such a way that the mathematics problem becomes relevant because the child sees himself or herself as part of the context.

Mathematical literary criticism and editing attempts to accomplish this by presenting children with problems that become "part of an ongoing web of intrigue that forms our lives" and arise within a "continuous context that gives students reason to find out more, to press for details, and to gain a lasting understanding" (Snyder, 1991, p. 7) both because the problem solutions have real consequences in their lives and because they tap into their fantasy life through association with a good children's story. For example, at the editing level, *The Doorbell Rang* becomes relevant to children's lives because they become editors of a book that they will actually alter and improve and then read to younger children. Here editing the book and reading to younger children become part of the "ongoing web of intrigue" that encompasses and has real consequences in children's lives. At the level of reader of the book, *The Doorbell Rang* taps into children's fantasy because most children can identify with the consequences of having to share a prized object with a friend and because the language and illustrations of the story build toward a rhythmic, suspenseful finale that offers consequences for its characters with which most children can identify. In doing so, the book draws children into its story and helps them imagine themselves as actors in the story. Thus when children confront mathematics in the story, the mathematics becomes a part of their fantasy world: It becomes their problem, not someone else's.

Involvement. Mathematical exercises and word problems usually do not entice children to become personally involved with them because they are not good stories, because they are usually temporally and situationally decontextualized from children's lives, and because children frequently have to solve numerous thematically different exercises at a single sitting, over a short period of time. Mathematical literary criticism and editing attempts to entice the child to become personally involved in the endeavor at two levels. At the level of reading the story, children become involved because the story is sufficiently rich to tap into their fantasy lives in ways that make it relevant to them. At the level of editing the story, when a child is given the chance to change a published book (by doing such things as altering its text, adding equations or diagrams, or elaborating upon illustrations in ways that actually have a significant impact on the book) and report those changes to significant people (such as peers, younger children, or the author), the child is exercising real mathematical and literary power in ways that stimulate the child to become personally involved, invested, and immersed in the process of mathematical literary criticism and editing.

A Problem-Solving Environment and Curricular Integration

The instructional environment underlying mathematical literary criticism and editing is based on the unit approach to instruction. Its major attributes are listed in Figure 3.3. In comparison, the instructional model underlying traditional mathematics instruction might be called the separate subject, direct instruction, lesson approach. These two models are very different.

The unit approach was first popularized by William Heard Kilpatrick (1918) in *The Project Method*, his interpretation of John Dewey's approach to education, and extended and redefined numerous times since then. In essence, the unit approach views instruction as contexts, environments, or units containing activities that have open-ended problems for children to engage and from which they can make meaning for themselves, as compared to viewing instruction as laying out content and skills to be learned by the child, who demonstrates the acquisition of the subject matter through replicating what was learned by achieving well on tests.

Two of the main assumptions of the unit approach are "instruction as an environment for learning" and "curricular integration." Elaborating on these two attributes as they relate to *The Doorbell Rang* example helps clarify two major assumptions of the instructional environment of mathematical literary criticism and editing.

A Problem-Solving Environment for Learning. The unit approach to mathematical literary criticism and editing is thought of as "a learning environment" that contains activities in which children engage in order to make meaning for themselves. The instructional environment, the sequence of activities that take place within it, and the types of activity in which children engage are largely defined by the enhanced version of Polya's problem-solving model discussed earlier in this chapter.

FIGURE 3.3. Attributes of the unit approach to mathematical literary criticism and editing

---

- A unit is thought of as "an environment" in which children learn that contains activities in which they engage in order to make meaning for themselves, rather than an organized body of concepts and skills laid out to be acquired by children.
- The intellectual environment created by the literary experience that is at the heart of the program provides the reason for children to develop mathematical and literary understandings, abilities, and attitudes.
- Knowledge is thought of as being holistically integrated across different areas of intellectual concern and not atomistically partitionable into distinct, separate academic subjects.
- Mathematics and literary criticism are viewed as relevant to and useful in children's daily lives, as well as exciting, fun, real, and enriching to engage in, both in the classroom and at home.
- Instruction is based on developmentally appropriate practice (the use of manipulatives, hands on experiences, starting with concrete meanings and moving toward abstractions, integrating the relationships between content areas, etc.).
- Students are grouped in different ways: as a whole class, in small groups, and as individuals.
- Assessment of student understanding is accomplished by examining their actual work in a variety of ways, including observing children at work, questioning them, discussing concepts with them, and examining their drawings, writings, and other creations.
- Scheduling is flexible, with activities sometimes extending over several days and with different parts of an activity sometimes being engaged in at several times during a single day.
- The unit lasts for an extended period of time (often weeks), not just an hour or so.
- Students work collaboratively in such a way that they have responsibility for the success of the learning experience, because success originates from a genuine need to work together.
- A unit is designed to teach problem solving as well as mathematics and literary criticism.
- Students get highly intellectually and emotionally involved with a unit, and this high involvement promotes increased effort and motivation.
- Students learn through a variety of types of communication including reading, listening, writing, talking, dramatizing, and drawing.
- The teacher's role is a complex one that includes adjusting the unit to the needs of the children being taught; designing and presenting the environment for learning; and overseeing children's work by listening, observing, responding, guiding, questioning, facilitating, and assessing their understandings while inspiring task-related conversation, reflection, understanding, and activity.

With the unit approach, a classroom frequently looks quite different from the separate subject, direct instruction, lesson approach classroom in that the solving of a single large, complex problem is at the center of instructional activity rather than the acquisition of concepts and skills that are exercised through the solving of multiple relatively simple separate exercises. The classroom is also distinguished from traditional mathematics and literature classrooms in that students are grouped in a variety of different ways, students work collaboratively, students rather than the teacher are usually at the center of activity, the teacher serves as a designer of activities and facilitator of student learning rather than as a deliverer of truth and manager of student practice exercises, and assessment is done through examining the actual literary and mathematical creations of children rather than through tests.

In mathematical literary criticism and editing, the scheduling of activities is temporally flexible. Sometimes activities last for several days, sometimes children engage in an activity several times during a single day, and some activities last for only a few minutes while others last for many hours. Activities are defined not by 30-, 40-, 50-, or 60-minute periods, but rather by the length of time that it takes to complete an endeavor. Teachers who usually have specified times for mathematics, reading, and language arts have been known to combine all three periods into a single block of time in order to flexibly schedule activities. One reason why scheduling is flexible is because instruction is viewed as consisting of holistic activities rather than content that can be partitioned into atomistic pieces, each of which defines a lesson and which can be learned separately. The temporal flexibility of mathematical literary criticism and editing can be observed within *The Doorbell Rang* example, where three or more activities are sometimes scheduled in a single day while at other times a single activity lasts for several days.

Curricular Integration. An important function of mathematical literary criticism and editing is that it fosters curricular integration by helping children simultaneously develop in the areas of both mathematics and literature.

Much has been written about curricular integration by those who advocate linking mathematics and literature. Unfortunately, most attempts to "integrate" mathematics and literature involve attempts to integrate a collection of objects—children's books—into an area of study—mathematics. There is usually no intention of integrating the subject areas of mathematics and children's literature. For most educators, such integration involves using children's books as springboards to launch the study of well-defined mathematical topics, and once the study of mathematics is launched the children's books are left behind. Here children's books are viewed as "objects" whose primary function is to facilitate mathematical learning (even if secondary language arts benefits are spoken about because children have to talk, write, read, or draw in order to communicate mathematical discoveries or information).

In contrast, during mathematical literary criticism and editing, two subject areas are being combined as equal partners in such a way as to simultaneously encourage both children's mathematical and literary development. Four aspects of integration need highlighting.

First, within mathematical literary criticism and editing, a literary experience that embodies mathematics—that is, a children's trade book that contains mathematics—lies at the heart of the instructional endeavor, and it is out of the mathematical literary experience that children develop both mathematical and literary meanings. This is in contrast to having mathematics arise within the context of a study of mathematical topics and having literary topics arise within the context of a study of literature. For example, *The Doorbell Rang* provides the intellectual experience from which children develop both mathematical and literary understandings, skills, and appreciations.

Second, in the problem-solving environment of mathematical literary criticism and editing, knowledge is holistically integrated across different areas of intellectual concern, not disintegrated into separate academic subjects. Mathematics and literature are not treated as two disjoint and dissimilar areas of study. It is believed that children can simultaneously construct mathematical and literary understandings while working on a single problem originating in both mathematical and literary concerns. In *The Doorbell Rang* example, children learn mathematics (and literary criticism) while engaging in the editorial endeavor of understanding a piece of literature, and they engage in the language arts activities of reading, writing, and speaking (as well as learning mathematics) while constructing their evolving mathematical meanings.

Third, "simultaneous" learning in both mathematics and literature is possible largely because children repeatedly visit a book during the endeavor, with interspersed discussions and activities. Children's increasingly heightened understanding of a book's mathematics allows them to obtain an increasingly better understanding of its story, while their ever greater understanding of a book's story allows them to become increasingly aware of how mathematics functions within it. Without the repeated revisiting of a book, this escalating ability of mathematical and literary growth to further stimulate each other could not easily exist.

Fourth, the issue of the balance of intended mathematical versus literary benefits for the child who engages in activities emphasizing the mathematics and children's literature connection is crucial. Of course, there need be no balance of benefits. Children's trade books that contain mathematics can be beneficially used solely as children's literature, ignoring their mathematics (as is usually the case in reading, language arts, or literature classes), or solely as springboards into mathematics, ignoring their literary components (as is usually the case in mathematics class). In mathematical literary criticism and editing, however, children's books can be used to help children acquire a somewhat balanced set of both mathematical and literary benefits.

Underlying the discussion of curricular balance is an issue raised by Charles De Garmo (1895) during the great debate about the correlation of school subjects during the middle of the 1890s—namely, what are the interrelationships between subjects that are connected or integrated within the school curriculum? De Garmo was concerned that if there was a superficial or artificial association between school subjects, or if one field of study was subordinated to another, then there would be no true unification of the knowledge of the two subjects and no balance of benefits accruing to both subjects. The belief was that the benefits that could accrue to the child from the true unification of two subjects would likely be far greater than the benefits that accrued from using the objects of one field of knowledge to motivate children to study another field of knowledge. From our present perspective, much of the movement to "integrate" or "link" mathematics and literature has unfortunately fallen into the trap that De Garmo warned us of more than a century ago, since it uses the objects (children's books) of one field of knowledge to motivate children to study another field of knowledge (mathematics). Hopefully mathematical literary criticism and editing, which presents one model of how the study of mathematics and literature can be integrated with a balance of benefits accruing to both areas of study, will stimulate the development of other models of doing so.

Several benefits accrue when mathematical literary criticism and editing simultaneously helps children develop both their mathematical and literary abilities. From a general curricular perspective, there is an enormously economical use of time when the two subjects are studied simultaneously and children's growth in two areas is simultaneously encouraged. From a literary perspective, children's understanding and enjoyment of a book (and literature as a whole) can be increased because children have both literary and mathematical ways of approaching it. From a mathematical perspective, children's understanding and enjoyment of a mathematical topic can be increased because children can associate the topic with a meaningful and fun literary experience. From an instructional perspective, children's discussions of either literature or mathematics can enrich the instructional arena in both of these areas because children can bring to the discussions both a mathematical and a literary perspective. From the perspective of the child's development, ways of constructing meaning within the literary and mathematical domains can enrich each other and provide a child with a more fully coordinated view of how to approach both mathematical and literary problems and issues in the future. From the perspective of relating children's in-school learning and out-of-school lives, children are encouraged to view both mathematics and literature as relevant components of human knowledge that relate to everyday events.

"CHILDREN'S LITERARY CRITICISM" AND "MATHEMATICAL LITERARY CRITICISM AND EDITING"

Children's literary criticism and mathematical literary criticism and editing share much in common. To explore possible relationships between the two, four concepts will be examined: the components and dynamics of the two approaches, literary context, constructivism, and the importance of story.

Components of the Literary Criticism Cycle

In *The Child as Critic*, Glenna Davis Sloan (1991) presents a comprehensive definition of children's literary criticism as an endeavor "that includes experiencing literature, responding to it, reflecting on it, and creating it" (p. 180). This broad definition identifies four interconnected activities that take place during literary criticism. Each will first be described from the perspectives of children's literary criticism and mathematical literary criticism and editing. Then, the dynamics among the activities will be explored as they occur during mathematical literary criticism and editing.

Experiencing. Whether as listener or reader, experiencing literature is the first step to be taken by a literary critic. It involves both engaging a piece of literature and having sufficient experience with a variety of types of literature that individual literary works can be related to the whole body of human literary endeavors.

Responding. Personally responding to the aesthetic experience of engaging a piece of literature is an important act for the literary critic. It involves making meaning as one lives through the literary experience. Responding can take the form of feelings aroused, questions raised, comments elicited, experiences evoked, or meanings stimulated in the child by the story that can either be shared with others or held private by the child. It involves the first responses of readers as they attempt to determine the effect of a piece of literature on themselves. It can involve the use of words, artistic images, physical acts, listening, or further reading. In responding, children can take an efferent or aesthetic stance (Rosenblatt, 1978). An efferent stance focuses readers' attention on the content or information in literature, while an aesthetic stance focuses readers' attention on the unique personal feelings, responses, images, associations, and thoughts evoked by the reading experience. Aesthetic responses are usually the preferred first responses for children (Sloan, 1991).

Reflecting. Reflecting on literature involves analyzing, relating, clarifying, critiquing, and evaluating a piece of literature that has been experienced. It involves relating a piece of literature to all of the other literature thus far experienced in terms of types of stories, setting and plot, characterization, point of view, mood or tone, style, message, symbolism, illustrations, and so forth. It involves imagining, theorizing, and hypothesizing about the structure and content of the story and its meaning to the author and the reader. Reflecting gives the critic greater understanding of, insight into, and appreciation of a particular literary work, literature as a whole, and the critic himself or herself. It also connects a literary critic to the knowledge that others have about literature by relating a literary critic's experience to the thoughts, feelings, and responses of others. It is what children do when they relate one book to another, comment on the roles that the hero and villain play in a story, compare the effect on the reader of the illustrations of two books, or question whether a book is a romance, tragedy, comedy, or satire.

Creating. In response to an encounter with literature, creating involves making an imaginative, reflective, critical, and creative comment that sums up the critic's responses to and reflections on the experience. Creating literature is an act of making literary meaning in a way that is intended to be shared with others. It is not just what scholars do when they write for learned journals or what reviewers do when they evaluate a book. It can involve oral expression, writing, dramatization, dance, music making, creative artwork, or some combination of these modes of expression. And each of these modes of expression can take a variety of forms. For example, writing can take the form of poetry, essays, storytelling, letters, or diaries. The creating of literature can involve a child working alone or in groups as children share their work by helping each other write, critique, revise, and rewrite their literary creations. It often involves the public display of a child's creation through oral presentation to a group, by putting it on exhibition, or through publication.

These four activities of literary criticism do not have to be distinct and separable endeavors, do not have to take place in a linearly sequential manner, can be revisited repeatedly during literary criticism, and can be interconnected. Much cycling between the activities of experiencing, responding, reflecting, and creating can take place as the process of literary criticism moves gradually from experience toward creation.

Components of the Mathematical Literary Criticism and Editing Cycle

When the four activities of the literary criticism cycle are examined as separate endeavors from the perspective of mathematical literary criticism and editing, two things can be discovered. First, within mathematical literary criticism and editing there exist parallel types of endeavors. Second, literary criticism's perspective on these four activities raises significant questions for the field of mathematics education. How the four literary criticism activities parallel activities within mathematical literary criticism and editing will now be briefly described, with reference to *The Doorbell Rang* example. One question related to each activity that literary criticism poses for mathematics education will also be raised.

Experiencing. In mathematical literary criticism and editing, experiencing encompasses two different areas: literature and mathematics. In *The Doorbell Rang* example, children encountered a story that led them to become immersed in both mathematical and literary experiences. The story, both as a book and as a mathematical dramatization, allowed children to encounter experiences in which human imagination and thought mingled in artistically pleasing ways. A question posed for mathematics educators by the field of literary criticism is: Are the ways in which we teach children mathematics going to give them the very best *artistic* experiences possible, experiences that will simulate both their *imagination* and *thought* about mathematics?

Responding. In mathematical literary criticism and editing, responding involves responding to the story as a piece of literature, responding to the mathematics imbedded in the story, responding to the quality of the story's presentation of its mathematics, and responding to the quality of the story's literary presentation. All of these were present in *The Doorbell Rang* example. In addition, readers responded in such a way as to make meaning first for themselves and then with a group by raising questions, generating comments and concerns, and recalling prior experiences and meanings. They responded with both an aesthetic and efferent stance, with the aesthetic stance coming first and leading into the efferent stance. A question posed for mathematics educators by the field of literary criticism is: Are the mathematical experiences that we provide children rich enough to call forth from children both pleasant aesthetic and meaningful efferent responses, and do we as educators encourage both types of responses?

Reflecting. In mathematical literary criticism and editing, reflecting involves analyzing, relating, clarifying, critiquing, and evaluating many things, including a book's mathematics and story, the effectiveness of a book's presentation of its mathematics and story, and the child's mathematical and literary meanings that relate to the book. This involves analyzing, theorizing, and hypothesizing about the book's mathematics and its story and the effectiveness of their presentation against a backdrop of all the mathematics the child is aware of and all the literature the child has experienced. In *The Doorbell Rang* example, children were given an opportunity to reflect in these ways through both their analysis and dramatization of the book. Planning and carrying out a plan to revise the book also required reflection, as did dealing with feedback related to one's editing plans and endeavors from one's peers and teacher. Children were required to do some of their reflecting in cooperative groups, partly because doing so connects the child to other children's knowledge of the book and its mathematics and forces the child to relate his or her reflections to the reflections, thoughts, experiences, and responses of others. A question posed for mathematics educators by the field of literary criticism is: How often do we ask children to reflect on the mathematics they are learning by putting it in the context of all of their mathematical meanings and the mathematical meanings of the community in which they live?

Creating. In mathematical literary criticism and editing, creating includes having children construct or reconstruct many things, including their understanding of a book's mathematics, a view of themselves as literary critics, the book itself, and their view of the problem-solving process. In *The Doorbell Rang* example, children examined the meaning of division and were asked to rethink, reconstruct, and give new meaning to their prior understanding of division. They were asked to act as and think of themselves as literary critics and editors. Also, children created edited versions of the book, letters describing their thoughts about the book, and reflections on the problem-solving process in which they had engaged. The creation process also included a chance for children to exhibit their books, to make an oral presentation describing how and why they edited their book, and to read their book to younger children. A question posed for mathematics educators by the field of literary criticism is: How often do we allow children to *create* and *share with others* either mathematical constructs that are new to them or new ways of presenting the mathematical meanings that they have created for themselves?

Of major importance in mathematical literary criticism and editing is the child's creative act of actually changing the piece of literature that initiated his or her literary experiences, responses, reflections, and creations. In most versions of children's literary criticism, there is only a one-way action that takes place when a child "interacts" with a book: The book influences the child by stimulating the child to make meaning; the child never acts back on the book in a significant way. In mathematical literary criticism and editing, a two-way action takes place when a child "interacts" with a book: the book acts on the child by stimulating changes in the child's meanings, and the child acts back on the book by enhancing it and, as a result, changing its meanings. The differences between two-way and one-way "interactions" are of major significance. Two-way "interactions" truly are interactions with two elements mutually influencing each other. In addition, two-way "interactions" give the child the same power of "changing the book's meaning" as the book has over the child, while in one-way "interactions" only the book has the power to influence the child.

Dynamics of the Mathematical Literary Criticism and Editing Cycle

The dynamics of mathematical literary criticism and editing are significantly more complex than those of literary criticism, because its activities are more complex and because each type of activity is cyclically revisited repeatedly. *The Doorbell Rang* example provides an illustration of how the relationships among the activities of experiencing, responding, reflecting, and creating function over time in mathematical literary criticism and editing. These dynamics are portrayed in Figure 3.4 and described in the following subsections.

FIGURE 3.4 **Dynamics of the mathematical literary criticism and editing cycle**
In each successive phase of the activity, the major emphasis (heavier part of the arrows) progresses to a different level of involvement for the students.

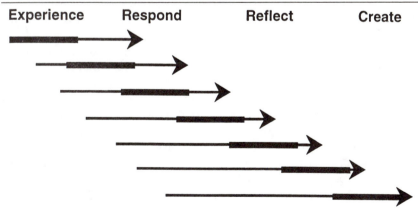

| Experience | Respond | Reflect | Create |

Experiencing. Mathematical literary criticism and editing begins by providing children with an experience with a book. They first have literary experiences and then mathematical experiences. As time passes, children continue to have experiences as the book is repeatedly reread. They also experience the responses and reflections of their peers, teachers, and themselves to the book. Eventually children experience the responses and reflections of their peers, teachers, and themselves to their creations and the creations of others.

Responding. Children respond to the experiences they have. In the beginning they respond to the book as a piece of literature. Later they respond to its mathematics and to their peers' responses to its mathematics. As the exploration of the book continues, children respond to their own preconceptions about the book's mathematics; the new mathematical experiences they have as they reflect on the book's mathematics; the book's literary elements; and their own reflections on their experiences, responses, and creative endeavors.

Reflecting. Children reflect on the responses they have to their experiences. At first they reflect on the book as a piece of literature and how the book relates to their previous experiences and other books. They also reflect on the responses to the book by their peers and teacher. Later children reflect on the book's mathematics, their own initial understanding of that mathematics, their growing understanding of that mathematics as they have new mathematical experiences, their responses to the adequacy of the book's presentation of its mathematics and literary elements, and the thoughts of their peers and teacher about these things. As children begin to create an edited version of the book, they reflect more deeply on the meaning of the book's mathematics, the way in which the book presents its mathematics and story, their revision of the book, the adequacy of their peers' revisions of the book, and their peers' and teacher's responses to their creative endeavors.

Creating. Children build their creations out of their reflections on their responses to their experiences. They build many significant creations: their own reconstructed view of mathematics; their view of themselves as literary critics; their revised version of the book; their thoughts about the process of problem solving they encounter; and their critical literary perspectives that allow them to more effectively experience, respond to, and reflect on future books they read. Children also construct new creations based on their peers' and teacher's responses and reflections to their own creations. Children's creations thus become one of the sources for experience that leads to responses, reflections, and future creations.

HERE THE LITERARY CYCLE—of experience leading to response, which leads to reflection, which leads to creation—is initiated repeatedly as a children's book is repeatedly visited from different perspectives, with the essence of the cycle continually moving from experience through response and reflection toward creation. These dynamics are similar to those of the spiral curriculum as each of the activities of experience, response, reflection, and creation is repeatedly revisited at ever more reflective and creative levels as the overall nature of activity moves from experience through response and reflection toward creation. Frequently the four endeavors merge into a single integrated experience that cannot be separated into distinct dis-integrated activities. Children often operate at a variety of intellectual levels during a single activity, as is the case when they are simultaneously creating a revised book, a reconstructed view of mathematics, and a perception of themselves as mathematicians, literary critics, and editors.

Three things are critical to note about the dynamics of mathematical literary criticism and editing that set it apart from almost all other methods of linking, connecting, or "integrating" two subjects.

First, most educators who write about the connection between mathematics and children's literature characterize it as involving only one or two encounters with a book. During mathematical literary criticism and editing, a book is returned to many times, with children thinking about the book and acting on it differently each time they reexamine it. Thus the interactions between the story and the child can grow, with each successive reading building on previous readings as the child's escalating mathematical and literary understandings further stimulate growth in each other.[1] This occurred in *The Doorbell Rang* example when children's increasingly greater understanding of the book's mathematics allowed them to obtain an increasingly better understanding of both its story and mathematics, and when their ever greater understanding of its story allowed them to become increasingly aware of how the mathematical and literary elements functioned within it.

Second, the predominant view of those promoting the connection between mathematics and literature is that literature is a springboard for introducing children to mathematics (Kliman, 1993; Welchman-Tischler, 1992). A springboard is a device that catapults a gymnast into the air or a swimmer first into the air and then into water; that is, a person is propelled from one medium into another in such a way that the person leaves behind the springboard upon entering the second medium. Most approaches to connecting mathematics and children's literature view children as entering a children's book for the primary purpose of being propelled into mathematics, and in the process of thus being propelled they leave behind the book. The view seems to be that "children's literature can be a starting point for looking at mathematics in a new way" (Whitin & Wilde, 1992, p. 2) and that such is sufficient. In contrast, during mathematical literary criticism and editing a book is returned to repeatedly, thus allowing children to embrace both its mathematical and literary dimensions in a balanced way. Because a book is revisited repeatedly, literature is viewed as something that children *dive into* in order to encounter both mathematics and literature rather than something that children are *propelled out of* in order to encounter mathematics.

Third, most educators who write about the connection between mathematics and children's literature would endorse the idea that "literature is a valuable mathematics tool" (Kolakowski, 1992, p. 5). It is seen as a tool in the hands of the teacher to help children learn mathematics and thus as an instrument to be used for a purpose separate from its own essence. Just as a cement mixer used in building a house is not part of the house once it is built, literature used in the context of helping children learn mathematics does not have a place within the mathematics learnings constructed by the children once the learning act has been completed. Literature is simply viewed as a tool whose value and purpose are secondary and only incidental to the mathematical structures constructed by children. But in mathematical literary criticism and editing, the relationship between mathematics and children's literature is viewed as having both literary and mathematical benefits. Children's literature helps children understand mathematics and mathematics helps children understand literature; children's mathematical and literary development take place simultaneously.

Literary Context

A major issue that literary criticism must deal with is the way in which a book can take on different meanings for different readers. This is partially explained by the concept of literary context, which holds that there are three major contextual factors that must be dealt with in the attempt to understand, appreciate, and evaluate a children's book and the effect that it has on readers: the meanings that readers bring to a book and their ability to make meaning out of interactions with it; the setting within which and the purposes for which a book is read; and the relationship that the book has to other children's books the reader has encountered. Exploring these three aspects of literary context will provide insight into the nature of mathematical literary criticism and editing.

The Reader. This first of the contextual factors is significant because it is the reader who makes meaning and it is within the reader that meanings reside. The meanings that a reader brings to a book, the meaning structures that allow the reader to put a book within a meaningful context, and the meaning-making ability of the reader all play a major role in determining how a book is understood, appreciated, and evaluated. Readers interpret books differently because "meaning is not 'contained' in the text, but is derived from an interaction between the content and structure of the author's message and the experience and prior knowledge of the reader" (Chase & Hynd, 1987, p. 531). Readers understand books differently because each reader is unique:

> As a reader, you bring to books . . . your attitude to books . . . your attitudes to life . . . your knowledge and experience of books . . . your knowledge and experience of life . . . your cultural background and prejudices . . . your race, class, age, and sex attitudes . . . and innumerable other minutiae of personality, background, and upbringing. These will all affect the way in which we make meaning: what we understand and what we take to be important. (Hunt, 1991, p. 70)

From the perspective of mathematical literary criticism and editing, the child's literary knowledge and experience, conceptions and misconceptions of mathematics, positive and negative feelings about mathematics and literature, understandings and misunderstandings of mathematics and literature, and prior experiences with mathematics and literature all play a role in the way in which a child understands, appreciates, evaluates, and enhances both a book and its mathematics. What is important is that one of the intents of mathematical literary criticism and editing is to alter these things in an attempt to help children develop their understanding and appreciation of mathematics and literature. In *The Doorbell Rang* example, children expose their understandings and misunderstandings of mathematics and literature to the teacher and peers during discussions so that they can be developed, elaborated upon, reinforced, or corrected. Having children confront and publicly describe their conceptions, feelings, and prior experiences with mathematics and literature in a nourishing environment is one way of helping them construct and reconstruct an adequate set of mathematical and literary meanings and feelings, and thus develop new ways of comprehending literature and mathematics.

Environment and Purpose. The setting in which and the purposes for which a book is read can greatly affect its meaning for a reader. Reading a book in school as part of an assignment likely provides a different experience than reading it for pleasure while settled into bed at night. Having a book read aloud by a parent in order to share a common experience can be very different from reading a book alone in a classroom of individuals who will soon be tested on their comprehension. Acknowledging this raises questions about the purpose and setting of mathematical literary criticism and editing.

Mathematical literary criticism and editing is an attempt to make sense of a book and its connection to the broader endeavors of mathematics, literary criticism, and the reader's own mathematical and literary meanings. A reader does so by reconstructing a book's mathematical and literary meanings, which involves such things as reading a book and thinking about it; talking about a book and listening to others speak about it; writing, drawing, graphing, and representing a book's messages, meanings, and extensions; or acting out a book's meanings through the manipulation of concrete embodiments or dramatizations. Doing so helps readers to construct, reconstruct, and clarify for themselves the book's meaning, mathematics, literature, themselves as individuals as well as mathematicians and literary critics, and the relationship among these things.

The setting in which this takes place requires two things of the child: (1) to enter the fantasy world of a book and (2) to pretend to be an editor of the book. The child continues to move in and out of these imaginary worlds and between them throughout.

Relationship to Other Books. Extremely important within literary criticism is the relationship that a book has to other books. As Northrop Frye (1963) says, "The critic's function is to interpret every work of literature in the light of all the literature he knows, to keep constantly struggling to understand what literature as a whole is about" (p. 44). One reason for doing this is articulated by Sloan (1991):

> An awareness of these relationships [among books] brings with it a sense of the significance of literature as the continuous journal of the human imagination, an interrelated body of imaginative verbal structures that examine every aspect of human experience, real or imagined. This awareness brings to the study of literature a sense of its immediate significance in our lives. (p. 35)

What is important here is the assumption that *an individual piece of literature can be better understood, appreciated, and evaluated if it is seen within its larger literary context rather than as an isolated element.* Mathematical literary criticism and editing attempts to apply this concept to mathematics as well. It is assumed that *a single mathematical fact, concept, or algorithm is better understood and appreciated if it is seen within the larger contexts of all mathematics and the real world of our daily lives, rather than as an isolated element.*

For example, at the most basic level, the arithmetic fact $3 + 2 = 5$ is better understood in the context of whole numbers from 1 to 10, in the broader context of the arithmetic on all numbers less than 100, and in the still broader context of all mathematical meanings than as an isolated number fact unto itself. It is even better understood in the very context of all of life (where things such as sharing cookies happen). Mathematical literary criticism and editing helps children understand and interpret a book's mathematics in both a larger mathematical context and a real-world context.

Constructivism

During the last decade constructivism has become a powerful philosophical force in education. Its origins date back at least to the eighteenth century, although its current popularity derives primarily from Piaget's writings. Constructivism rests on several assumptions: Knowledge cannot be separated from the process of meaning making—or knowing. Knowledge—or meaning—is created by learners out of an interaction between their prior meanings and new experiences that they have, rather than passively received by them and stored as mental images of objective reality. Meaning making—or knowledge construction—enables learners to adapt to their world by constructing subjective explanations for their experiences. And knowledge is personally constructed and socially mediated: Knowledge and knowing function in both social and individual contexts.

Constructivism In Literary Criticism. Most approaches to children's literary criticism assume that meaning does not reside in a piece of literature in and of itself, but that meaning is constructed by readers as they interact with a book through the process of reading it—or listening to it. An experience is assumed to be waiting for readers within a book, an experience out of which they will construct their own individual meanings and shared group meanings in accordance with their unique set of perceptions of the book's text, their prior experiences, their understandings of their world and system of organizing those understandings, and their purposes.

These constructivist assumptions derive from the work of developmental psychologists in general, from the work of reader-response theorists in the field of children's literature, and, most specifically, from Louise Rosenblatt's (1938; 1978; 1991) transactional theory of literary work:

> According to Rosenblatt, reading involves a transaction between the reader and the text wherein the reader constructs a personal envisionment of meaning guided by the blueprint offered by the text. During reading, readers draw on past experiences, select from various alternative referents to words and ideas, form images and associations, and savor feelings evoked by the text. Readers are guided by the text as they select, reject, and order meanings. (McGee, 1992, p. 530)

The meaning a reader constructs from an experience with a book is a function of the images the reader creates, the associations the reader makes, the questions the reader brings to a book, and the expectations aroused in the reader both before the book is encountered and while it is being read. The child's perceptual, affective, and intellectual activity is bound up with the creative process of making meaning from the book as he or she experiences the book and incorporates its graphic information and structural organization into an existing body of meanings, a conglomerate of intellectual meaning-making structures, a set of expectations, and literary interpretative predispositions relating to the mechanics of reading, the making of denotative and connotative meaning, the interpreting of literary allusions, and generic expectations of how texts work (Hunt, 1991).

Because children are viewed as "constructing meaning" rather than "getting meaning" from text, children's literary criticism moves beyond asking children to demonstrate literal recall of information from books; instead, they are asked to engage in critical analysis of, reflective thinking about, and imaginative and creative meaning-making about the experiences they encounter and the responses they have while reading a book. Among the instructional techniques that reader response theories suggest for implementing a constructivist approach to children's literature study are: reader response prompts, that is, teacher-provided questions that guide children's responses to literature (Kelly & Farnan, 1991; Many & Wiseman, 1992); grand conversations, in which teachers encourage children's comments as a way of facilitating enriched discussions out of which individual and group meaning is constructed (Eeds & Wells, 1989); and dialogue journals, in which teachers and students respond to each other in writing in a manner that allows for the sharing of experiences and reflections (Kelly & Farnan, 1991; McGee, 1992).

Constructivism in Mathematical Literary Criticism and Editing. Underlying mathematical literary criticism and editing is the same constructivist approach to meaning making that was just described for literary criticism. Its dynamics are presented in Figure 3.5.

At the center of the meaning-making process is the child, the meaning-maker. The child interacts with a book to construct meaning by experiencing it, responding to it, reflecting on it, and using it as the starting point for a creation.

The child also constructs meaning by interacting with peers through discussions in which children use various forms of language (verbal, written, diagrammatic, etc.) to share meanings, clarify thoughts, and test the adequacy of understandings related to the book that they are working with. These interactions take place in cooperative learning groups because the social setting allows children to construct and share meaningful verbalizations with others and to listen to the verbalizations that others share back in response. This is one purpose of the small group dramatizations of *The Doorbell Rang,* during which children read, act, write, speak, observe, and monitor each

FIGURE 3.5 Constructivist dynamics of mathematical literary criticism and editing

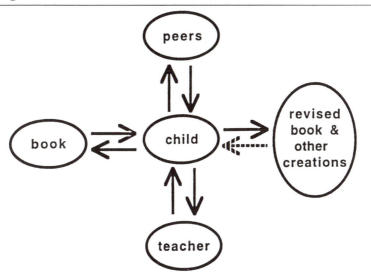

other's mathematical expressions. Cooperative learning groups also allow children to construct group as well as individual and meaning.

The child also interacts with the teacher, who plays a critical role, to obtain guidance while exploring the book, to share meanings, to clarify reflections, to test hypotheses generated, and to model behavior. It is the teacher who constructs the physical, affective, social, and intellectual environment in which the child constructs meaning.

Finally, the child produces a revised book out of this meaning-making experience. Revising a book—and creating the intellectual constructs that accompany it—can be conceptualized as a creative and artistic expression of meaning by children that summarizes and highlights for them the experiences encountered and new meanings constructed.

Within this model, children's new experiences, responses, and reflections must be coordinated with their prior accumulation of meanings and meaning-making structures through the processes of assimilation and accommodation. In addition, children's interactions with a book, peers, and the teacher both helps children understand the book and its connection to the broader endeavors of mathematics and literary criticism and helps them understand and extend their own mathematical and literary meanings.

Central to mathematical literary criticism and editing are the same techniques discussed in the previous section on Constructivism in Literary Criticism: reader response prompts (the questions that guide children's first responses to *The Doorbell Rang*, such as "What was important in the book and why?"); grand conversations (in which the teacher seizes on children's comments to highlight issues, such as the role of division, to facilitate discussions from which both individual and group meanings are constructed); and dialogue journals (the children's journals in which the teacher responded to children's writing).

Interactions Between a Reader and a Book. It has generally been assumed that when a child reads or is read to, the child will use the new experiences from the encounter with the book to make new meanings by combining previously accumulated meaning and the new experiences obtained from the book. This is often described as the process of making meaning from the introduction of a new experience that "stimulates" assimilation and accommodation to take place "within the child's mind." What is noteworthy about this model of learning is that it is assumed that the book will act on the child but that the child will not act on the book (except that the child will reconstruct the meaning of the book within his or her own mind).

But why do the interactions between a child and a book have to be one-way events? Why is the child never given a chance to act on the book in such a way that the book is changed? Some advocates of the connection between mathematics and children's literature do suggest that children alter books in a modified way. For example, Burns (1992b) suggests that children write their own books as a result of being inspired by a particular children's book, Sheffield (1995) suggests that children discuss the consequences of changing the number and type of items used within a book, and Burk, Snider, and Symonds (1991) suggest that children reenact a book's events through a dramatic production. However, in all of these cases the child's creative response to a piece of literature leaves that piece of literature unchanged. The same is the case in the field of children's literary criticism: As a result of "interacting" with a book, children are changed but the book remains unchanged.

Why have children not been urged to apply pencil, crayon, scissors, glue, or stapler to a book in such a way that the child's creative response to a book results in the book itself being changed? If the book is entitled to change the child's mind, why is the child not entitled to change the book?

Most of the common uses of the word *interaction* involve both the parties in an interaction being changed. *Webster's New Collegiate Dictionary* (1991) defines interaction as "mutual or reciprocal action or influence." But educators who write about the connection between mathematics and literature or about children's literary criticism never highlight these mutual influences, and the reason for this is simple: It is assumed that a book will act on a child but that no reciprocal interaction will take place (except for the inter-actions that take place within the child's mind as the child creates meaning out of the actions to which he or she has been subjected). Fortunately, other assumptions are possible.

In mathematical literary criticism and editing, the relationship between the reader and the book is framed as one of interaction: The book changes the reader and the reader changes the book. The book acts on the child, by stimulating changes in the child's meanings, and the child acts back on the book by enhancing it and, as a result, changing its meanings. The signifi-cance of this is great, for it gives children an enormously greater sense of mathematical and literary power than does a learning environment in which only the reader can be changed by a book.

It should be noted that underlying some of the current CD-ROM versions of "interactive" children's books is an attempt to set up a learning environ-ment in which a child can act on a book's text or pictures and the book itself responds by transforming itself in some predefined way. Here the book acts on the reader's meanings and the reader acts on the computer's presentation of its text and illustrations. Children can get very excited about the power they have over the computerized book, and that power itself can create major transformations in some children while they are engaged with the computer. Problems exist, however, with interactive CD-ROM books: They are usually viewed by children as short, gamelike activities rather than serious explora-tions of mathematical and literary issues; the range of actions that the reader can perform on the books are usually very limited; and the types of interac-tions usually involve only the child and the computer, rather than including the book, child, peers, and teacher. However, the medium holds great promise for the future.

The Importance of Story

Many children's books narrate a story. In doing so, the best ones do far more than simply tell a story: Stories—particularly narrative fantasies—offer us a safe way of exploring our world and articulating its meaning to our-selves, of making coherent meaning out of the feelings and thoughts that are aroused by our world (Bettelheim, 1976, p. 24). What is important about narrative stories—be they stories in which imbalances are resolved, growth takes place, or thoughts are revealed—is that fictional narrative shares much

> with that inner and outer storytelling that plays a major role in our sleeping and waking lives. For we dream in narrative, remember, anticipate, hope, despair, believe, doubt, plan, revise, criticize, construct, gossip, learn, hate, and love by narrative. In order really to live, we make up stories about ourselves

and others, about the personal as well as the social past and future. (Hardy, 1977, p. 13)

From the perspective of literary criticism, the endeavors of listening to stories, reading stories, writing stories, telling stories, and imagining stories "are essentials in the child's development. Stories teach children to read and write. Stories help children make sense of their inner and outer worlds. Stories convince them that reading is worth doing" (Sloan, 1991, p. 107). Stories provide children with enjoyment. Stories motivate children to explore literature. Stories allow children to express themselves and communicate intimately with others who have expressed themselves. Stories allow the child to experience, respond, reflect, understand, empathize, imagine, wonder, question, and create in thoughtful and feeling ways. Stories allow children to imagine themselves as someone else and experience a reality other than their own. Stories allow children to observe and then model another person's behaviors, thoughts, or feelings. Stories, if read or listened to in abundance, "significantly improves children's vocabulary and reading comprehension, and results in greater complexity and sophistication of syntax in both oral and written language" (Sloan, 1991, p. 108).

In mathematical literary criticism and editing, the child plays two roles with respect to a book's story: The child steps into the story to live it (usually as one or more of its characters) and into the role of editor to enhance it, thus engaging the story at the level both of the actors who live within it and of the author who creates it. Engaging a story and its mathematics at these two levels is more demanding and rewarding than engaging a story at the former level alone.

From the perspective of mathematical literary criticism and editing, stories offer children many mathematical benefits (as well as the literary benefits mentioned above). Stories offer children effective ways to envision the meaning of mathematics in the context of human endeavors and the role that mathematics can play in human lives; beyond this, stories stimulate the emotions and the imagination. They allow children to step into someone else's shoes and acquire a taste for the enjoyment of doing mathematics and the feeling of power that it can give a person. They allow for mathematical endeavors to be tied to the human questions, wonderings, hopes, adventures, and fears that generate mathematical endeavors in the first place (Egan, 1986; Griffiths & Clyne, 1991). The very nature of stories makes them a far more personal and powerful medium for learning and expression than the medium of the mathematics textbook or worksheet, which tend to decontextualize mathematics from human life by dissociating mathematical understanding from human strivings, emotions, and imagination.

An excellent story also allows an author to speak to children in a way and on a level that is uniquely suited to children's way of making meaning.

Similarly, they allow children, as editors during mathematical literary criticism and editing, to speak to one another in a way and on a level that makes sense to them. Many developmental psychologists have commented on the ways in which children understand differently from adults. Piagetians, for example, describe children of elementary school age as being at the concrete operational stage of intellectual development, which means that they understand mathematics best when given concrete examples—examples involving specific situations or concrete physical manipulatives—upon which they can either act directly or envision themselves or another person acting. In other words, they are best capable of understanding in the context of specific well defined narrative situations where the actions being taken are concretely defined by a person's actions and their explanations of those actions. As a result, what young children understand best are not the generalized, logical, and abstract explanations of adults (which are consistent with Piaget's next stage of development) but rather narrative stories that describe how children (either themselves, other children, or other childlike creatures) do things or understand things in terms of a series of concrete and specific actions. For example, children are more likely to understand the concept of division in the context of a narrative story, such as *The Doorbell Rang,* when they must personally do such things as read the story about the distribution of cookies, act out the story's division problems using cookies, verbally comment on the division as it takes place, and record the division as it occurs than they are to understand division by logical reference to division as the "inverse of multiplication" or a process of "repeated subtraction" (two popular interpretations of the meaning of division).

Missing from most of the mathematical explanations given to children are excellent concrete stories—stories that show children how problems can be solved through a concrete set of specific actions, that explain why each action is taking place, that take place in a real-world or fantasy context in which the story's actors are resolving a real problem they have encountered during their adventures, and that stir the child's emotions, intellect, imagination, and curiosity. Providing children with such explanations and asking them to express such explanations themselves are among the functions of narrative stories within mathematical literary criticism and editing.

THE POWER AND FUNCTION OF LANGUAGE IN LEARNING MATHEMATICS

In *The Doorbell Rang* example, children use language in many ways as they work alone and in groups. They use language to listen to and read the book as they experience its story; to help them comprehend, formulate, and share their reactions to the book as they respond to it; and to help them analyze, clarify, understand, and share their experiences as they reflect on them. And they use both words and drawings to help them create a revised version of the book that expresses its potential mathematical and literary meanings more elegantly, specifically, and clearly than the original. *The use of language is essential during mathematical literary criticism and editing.* How language helps children learn mathematics will now be explored.

For children—indeed, for all humans—language plays an extremely powerful role in the creation and sharing of new ideas, meanings, and understandings. So powerful an intellectual tool is language that some have said it is more powerful than weapons, while others have questioned our ability to think rationally without words to formulate our thoughts.

Why is language considered to be such a powerful intellectual tool in facilitating children's mathematical growth, learning, understanding, and thinking? Why is language considered so central to children's endeavors to create new mathematical ideas, meanings, and understandings? Educators and philosophers have wondered about these questions. Key to understanding them is realizing that the language of mathematics helps humans to formulate, understand, and express ideas and thoughts about their world, and that our everyday language helps people learn, understand, and express their mathematical ideas.

In general, the power of language derives from its ability to help children make sense of their experiences—to see patterns, solve problems, make connections, reason logically, draw conclusions, have insights—and relate their experiences and their thoughts about those experiences to the cumulative experience of the culture that is encoded in the traditions, knowledge, symbols, and images of mathematics. By participating in the effort to formulate, clarify, explore, and express mathematical meanings and insights, children both come to better understand those meanings and insights and to learn to use mathematical language and knowledge with increasing competence, ease, and precision.

Central to the question of the power of language during mathematical literary criticism and editing—and in the learning of mathematics and thinking about mathematics in general—is the question of the relationship between thought and language. Currently there are at least three popular positions among educators: Language and thought are identical and whenever one occurs the other is present; language and thought are independent of each other, with one being subordinate and one being the stimulus that initiates the other; and language and thought are separate endeavors that are interconnected in such a way that they continually interact with each other and influence each other (Parker & Goodkin, 1987). In all cases, language and thought are viewed as inextricably linked intellectual activities that mutually influence each other. Within this context, the power of language resides in its ability to facilitate thought, both as a result of individual reflection and construction of meaning and as a result of interpersonal and sociocultural communication. From this perspective, it is through language that all the benefits of human thought accrue to us as individuals and to humankind as a whole.

To describe the roles that language plays in mathematical literary criticism and editing, six distinctions will be made to set the stage for describing some of the roles of language in learning and understanding mathematics.

Language and Learning

A distinction needs to be made between learning about the language of mathematics, learning the language of mathematics, and learning mathematics through the use of language. All three of these types of learning are important within mathematical literary criticism and editing.

When studying mathematics, children learn about the language of mathematics. For example, in *The Doorbell Rang* example, children learn that different types of division signs exist.

When studying mathematics children learn to use the language of mathematics. For example, in *The Doorbell Rang* example, they learn to say the appropriate mathematical verbalizations and write the appropriate mathematical symbols that correspond to the mathematical event of sharing 12 cookies equally among 6 children.

When studying mathematics, children learn mathematics through the use of language, whether the language being used by them is everyday language or mathematical language. In *The Doorbell Rang* example, children learn that division must involve sharing equally among the children receiving cookies, as a result of participating in a discussion about this during which incorrect views are expressed, clarified, and corrected. This third type of learning is of critical importance. *Understanding that children can learn mathematics through the use of language is crucial to understanding the power of language in the learning of mathematics.*

Language, Expression, and Meaning-Making

A distinction needs to be made between using language to express ideas for the benefit of others and using language to formulate and express one's own thoughts to and for oneself. Children can use written, spoken, and gestural language to communicate their ideas to others. This occurs many times in *The Doorbell Rang* example: when children share their responses to the first several readings of the book with the teacher and each other, when children demonstrate their ability to imitate the language and actions modeled by the teacher during the book's dramatization, and when children enhance the book.

Children can also use oral, written, and gestural language as a way of generating thoughts for themselves. Children often use oral articulation as they search for their own meanings by attempting to access their thoughts and put them into words that they themselves can reflect on, organize, clarify, analyze, evaluate, and discover how to express in the most beautiful and eloquent way possible—so that they themselves can better understand their own meanings. This can be done either alone or with others. Writing also provides children with a way of coming to understand their own thoughts by helping them find words to express thoughts that might never have been expressed before, thoughts that can be reflected upon, clarified, organized, analyzed, and evaluated only after they have been put in a written form that can be objectively examined. Much of the use of language in *The Doorbell Rang* example was to first give children experiences and then to ask them to find words to express the meaning of those experiences for themselves, that is, to think for themselves. Children think as they talk and write, and by asking them to talk and write we can ask them to think by creating meanings for themselves.

Knowledge, Skills, Meaning, and Language

A distinction needs to be made among the use of language to transmit knowledge, to develop skills, and to aid in the construction of meaning. Language can facilitate many different types of learning. It can transmit knowledge or information from one person to another: from a teacher to a child, from a child to a peer, or from a child to the teacher. It can help children develop skills or condition their behavior—be it physical behavior, symbol or number manipulation, or verbal abilities. Language can also help children construct meaning from their intuitions and experiences. All three uses of language occur in *The Doorbell Rang* example. However, it is the use of language to help children construct meaning that is of particular importance in this discussion.

Language and Constructing Meaning

A distinction needs to be made among the use of language to facilitate the construction of meaning as a result of looking into oneself to subverbal meanings, looking into oneself to meanings that have already been brought to consciousness through language, and looking to new experiences.

Many believe that children have a reservoir of personal meanings existing just below the surface of their consciousness that are both an enormous resource to them and an enormous influence on them. It is believed that many of these subverbal meanings can be transformed into conscious meanings when words, phrases, sentences, symbols, equations, and other mathematical or nonmathematical representations are found to express them. One way of viewing children's endeavors when they are writing or speaking is that they are thinking out loud as they attempt to discover the meanings within themselves that have previously not been articulated or consciously understood. It is only when the thoughts are expressed that the child can turn back on the newly objectifiable expressions to reflect upon, clarify, organize, analyze, and test them against experience and the reactions of others. This is much of what *The Doorbell Rang* example is about: It encourages children to look into their subconscious meanings about mathematics so that those meanings can be brought to a verbal level, where they can be reflected on, elaborated, clarified, organized, analyzed, and tested against real-world experience.

When children use language to reconsider their own thoughts that have been brought to consciousness through language, they are also frequently engaged in the process of constructing meaning. When a child writes or articulates a thought that has already been verbalized and accepted as truth, then reconsiders that thought, and finally rephrases the thought, the child is involved in constructing new meanings for himself or herself through the use of language. The new language (as a carrier of the new meanings) might be constructed for a variety of reasons, including discovering an inconsistency, discovering a connection to another thought, reorganizing a set of thoughts, seeking to express a thought more eloquently, or attempting to bring more clarity to a thought. Again, this is much of what *The Doorbell Rang* example is about: putting children in a situation in which they reconsider their understanding of mathematics and, in so doing, reconstruct and enlarge that understanding.

Language also enables children to make meaning by helping them to make sense out of new experiences. Reading a new book, dealing with feedback from a peer or teacher related to work done, or confronting a new social interaction, and then attempting to find words that give meaning to the book's language, the feedback, or the social interaction, involves using language to help construct meaning out of new experiences.

Feedback from a teacher or peers through verbal or written interaction is a particularly powerful form of new experience for children that allows them to test the adequacy of their ideas through the linguistic processes of speaking and listening, or writing and reading. Feedback allows children to obtain information about the adequacy of their ideas, new information related to their thoughts, and guidance that directs, reorients, or facilitates their construction of new ideas. In *The Doorbell Rang* example, one reason children are put in social groups is so that, by verbally monitoring each other's expressions and providing each other with feedback about those expressions, they are stimulated to construct new meanings. One reason that children write in dialogue journals that are responded to by teachers is so that the written feedback can stimulate them to reconsider their original words (and thoughts). Here the written interactions provide children with new linguistic experiences that allow them to reevaluate their original meanings and construct new ones.

These three uses of language are not disjoint: Meanings not yet verbalized, meanings already verbalized, and meanings arising from new experiences are always in dynamic interaction. For example, when, in *The Doorbell Rang* example, children are confronted with the new experience of the book, verbally express their thoughts about a subject such as how division relates to events in the story, have those thoughts evaluated and responded to by a peer or teacher, and then reconsider and reformulate those thoughts themselves before expressing them again, they are using language to help themselves construct meaning by assimilating and accommodating new experiences relating to the book, previously held meanings at the subverbal and verbal levels, and new experiences from feedback given by others.

Social and Individual Uses of Language

A distinction needs to be made between the social and individual uses of language. Even though the previous paragraphs speak of language in individualistic terms, and even though individuals use language to form their own meanings and to learn, language must also be viewed as a sociocultural instrument. From a sociocultural perspective, in which learning is viewed as a sociocultural process and knowledge as a sociocultural construction, language is one of the major communication vehicles for expressing and sharing social knowledge in order to pass on the traditions of the culture to its members for the purposes of preserving, perpetuating, and extending the culture (Halliday, 1975; Vygotsky, 1978).

From this perspective, mathematics can be viewed as comprising a community of people interested in both creating mathematical meanings in new learners and creating new meanings in the field of mathematics. As a community, those interested in mathematics have: a tradition and a history; a body of agreed-upon knowledge and conceptual structures; a heritage of literature and artifacts; a specialized language of symbols, terms, functions, representational systems, and a grammar and logic for expressing ideas; a communications network; and a valuative and affective stance toward the world. Part of the function of language is to help novices become members of the community of mathematicians by learning all these components. Part of the power of language is that by learning the language of mathematics in the broadest sense, one acquires the power over the world that members of the field of mathematics as a whole have acquired over centuries of making mathematical meanings.

The sociocultural nature of language is evident in many parts of *The Doorbell Rang* example. The example begins with children sitting in a social group and listening to the reading of a communication from the book's author, which comes in the form of a story about the social interactions among a group of children. Throughout the unit, children meet in social groups in which they formulate their reactions and reflections in language, share them with the group, and receive feedback from the group. Children are drawn into the community of mathematical discourse as they learn the language of division while performing dramatizations—where they take turns as mathematical speaker, mathematical recorder, and mathematical manipulator of chips and plates in a social setting in which their developing language is monitored by the very group that is developing the shared language of division.

Language is performing a sociocultural function when the class as a whole gradually develops a common mathematical way of thinking about the book. Here language allows children to participate in a classroom community involved in mathematical discourse and develop shared mathematical understandings with others in their classroom. Here reading, writing, speaking, listening, and gesturing effect a meeting of minds and an interchange of ideas where readers or listeners must infuse meaning into another person's communication, and where writers or speakers must infuse meaning into language in such a way that readers or listeners can draw meaning from what was expressed.

Note that this sociocultural view of language is not intended to deemphasize the importance of the use of language by individuals, but rather to put individual endeavors in a sociocultural context.

Language and Levels of Mathematical Abstraction

A distinction needs to be made among the different levels of mathematical abstraction at which language can be used by children. Four different levels that are identifiable among a continuum of levels that lead from natural language to mathematical symbols are described below.

- *Natural Language Level.* Here children use their own everyday language to describe and think about mathematical situations or problems in the same manner as when referring to everyday events.
- *Concrete Representational Level.* Children use their own everyday language to describe and think about mathematical situations or problems

while referring to physical manipulatives, embodiments, or materials that represents them. Here children use natural language to monitor and describe their actions as they act out mathematical stories with physical embodiments.

- *Concrete Mathematical Level.* Children use mathematical language (terms, symbols, equations, or representational systems such as graphs, tables, and diagrams) to describe and think about a mathematical situation or problem while referring to a physical manipulative or visual image that represents it. Here children use mathematical language to monitor and describe their actions as they act out mathematical stories with either physical embodiments or intellectual images.
- *Symbolic Level.* Children use mathematical language to describe and think about mathematical situations or problems in abstract and generalizable terms. Here mathematical symbols and verbalizations are linked with abstract mathematical images as children use abstract thought to model, express, and construct mathematical meanings.

Most of these levels of mathematical language were present in *The Doorbell Rang* example. When the story was first discussed by children, they used natural language to describe its mathematical events. Later, concrete representational language was used when the story was performed by the class with physical manipulatives and children to represent its events. Shortly after this, concrete mathematical language was used when children performed variations of the story in small groups, while taking turns as story reader, mathematical commentator, mathematical recorder, and manipulator of mathematical embodiments.

An awareness of the different linguistic levels at which children think and communicate helps one "meet children where they are" in order to either facilitate their learning at their current linguistic level or facilitate their growth by asking them to communicate and think at a level slightly higher than is their norm.

Language can also be used at a *metacognitive level*, to help children think about their own cognitive processes. When children use language to gain insight into their own and other children's thinking processes, the sharing has the potential to help children see, understand, access, regulate, monitor, and orchestrate their own mathematical knowledge, skills, meanings, thinking processes, behaviors, attitudes, and feelings. Metacognition is facilitated by children's reflecting on and receiving feedback about their own and others' thoughts and thought processes. Metacognition is highlighted in mathematical literary criticism and editing when children "look back" on their endeavors and reflect on such things as their enhanced books, the problem-solving process in which they engaged, and younger children's concepts of mathematics.

The Role of Language in Learning and Understanding Mathematics

In summary, the above six distinctions lay the groundwork for comprehending some of the multiple roles that language plays during mathematical literary criticism and editing, as well as the power and function of language in helping children learn, understand, and use mathematics. Language—in the forms of reading, writing, speaking, listening, drawing, and gesturing—is a powerful mathematical tool for many reasons. The following are some of them.

Language helps children encounter mathematical experiences, be it with real-world problems, verbal or written communications from or with others, or reflections on their own conscious or subconscious mathematical meanings, thoughts, procedures, or intuitions.

Language helps children learn mathematics. It helps them learn mathematics by constructing new meanings, acquiring new understandings and information, and developing new skills.

Language allows children to express their mathematical ideas. Putting their mathematical thoughts into words or symbols allows them to discover, objectify, and confront their meanings. It allows children to better reflect on, organize, clarify, evaluate, comprehend, revise, and express their ideas. As a metacognitive tool, it helps children access, understand, monitor, and orchestrate their own mathematical constructs—and by so doing facilitates their enhancement, development, and reconstruction.

Language helps children enter the community of mathematical discourse and develop common shared mathematical understandings with others. Through language children learn to share the specialized language, knowledge, traditions, and affective stance of mathematics.

Language helps children personalize mathematics. It helps them relate new experiences to previous experiences in ways that facilitate assimilation and accommodation. The personalization helps reveal mathematics to be a human endeavor—relevant, meaningful, and useful in their everyday lives.

Language helps children understand, think about, and reflect on mathematics. Language—and the communication within a child or between a child and peers, a child and adult, or a child and text—facilitates children's reflections on their own mathematical meanings and other's mathematical communications. It helps children formulate conjectures and convincing arguments (or proofs). And it can focus a child's thoughts, particularly during the act of writing or speaking, in ways that enable a child to confront and transform existing mathematical meanings into new meanings. In so doing, writing or speaking enables the child to construct new meanings as the concepts, words, symbols, or representations used to express the thoughts are connected in new configurations that can produce new insights, discoveries, or rediscoveries of meaning.

Language helps children communicate their mathematical thoughts and allows them to construct and articulate mathematical meanings for themselves and to share them with others.

Language helps children remember mathematics. It can help children remember newly acquired mathematics by allowing them to summarize, organize, or personalize those meanings in their own words.

Language helps children assess mathematical ideas. It helps them assess their own thoughts by putting those thoughts into words that can be reflected on, analyzed, and evaluated. It helps them make use of feedback from others about the adequacy of their mathematical meanings, thoughts, behaviors, and feelings. It helps them evaluate the ideas of others through reading, listening, and observation.

Language helps children make connections: to see how mathematical ideas can be expressed in different ways; to link informal and intuitive mathematical meanings to more formal, abstract symbolism; to see connections among various forms of mathematical representation (oral, written, concrete, pictorial, numerical, graphical, algebraic, geometrical, etc.); to relate new mathematical experiences to previous ones; and to relate different areas of mathematical study to one another. It helps children see how their everyday language and experiences can relate to mathematics and how mathematical constructs can model real-world situations.

Language helps children relate mathematics and the worlds of the imagination and beauty. It helps children associate mathematics with the imaginative world of ideas in books, songs, poetry, and the arts. It helps children encounter the affective and aesthetic dimensions of mathematics. In so doing, it opens the doors to issues such as the beauty of clear and simple mathematical expressions or the elegance of proofs and demonstrations.

SUMMARY

Together, Chapters 2 and 3 have described a new pedagogical method—mathematical literary criticism and editing—for the integration of mathematics and children's literature and provided an analysis of some of the pedagogical and philosophical assumptions underlying that method. Its main purpose is to help people to better understand a book, themselves, mathematics, literary criticism, and the relationships among these four elements. During the process readers reconstruct a book's mathematical and literary meanings; reconstruct the book itself; construct, reconstruct, and clarify their own mathematical and literary meanings; and develop perceptions of themselves as mathematical problem solvers, literary critics, and editors. It takes place in a language-rich social environment for learning that centers on the endeavor of problem solving as children engage in the activities of experiencing, responding, reflecting, and creating.

The literature thus far published on the connection between mathematics and literature provides almost no serious discussion of the assumptions underlying new methodologies developed. This chapter has attempted to remedy this situation by presenting some of the philosophical and pedagogical assumptions underlying mathematical literary criticism and editing related to problem solving, literary criticism, and the power and function of language in learning mathematics. In a time when the connection between mathematics and literature is gaining popularity, others are invited to clarify the pedagogical and philosophical assumptions underlying the instructional methods they create. Hopefully a discussion of the philosophical and pedagogical assumptions underlying different approaches to linking mathematics and literature during instruction will lead to both greater understanding of possible linkages between the fields and to the generating of other new ways of linking the two fields of study.

4

Evaluation Standards for Children's Mathematics Trade Books

Currently, literary criticism that addresses children's trade books containing mathematics is not at all sophisticated, lacking, among other things, evaluation standards. Two distinct sets of standards are needed and have been developed—one addressing mathematical concerns (see Figure 4.1) and the other addressing literary issues (see Figure 4.2).

In this chapter I will discuss only mathematical standards, since adequate discussion of literary issues exists elsewhere. Suffice it to say that children's books need to be not only mathematically sound but also "good books" from a literary perspective.

Each of the mathematical standards will now be discussed, both to give concrete meaning to the standard and to help the reader see how it can be used to identify the comparative strengths and inadequacies of children's books. One standard—"A book should present an appropriate view of mathematics"—will be discussed in greater depth than the others to illustrate how specific criteria can be used to concretely define a standard, how several books can be comparatively assessed with respect to a standard, and how important it is to rate books in the context of other books with similar content and of the same genre.

A BOOK'S MATHEMATICS SHOULD BE CORRECT AND ACCURATE

Children's books must be assessed for the accuracy of their content. At the simplest level, they should not present incorrect calculations, algorithms,

FIGURE 4.1. Mathematics standards

- A book's mathematics should be correct and accurate.
- A book's mathematics should be effectively presented.
- A book's mathematics should be worthy of being learned.
- A book's mathematics should be visible to the reader.
- A book should present an appropriate view of mathematics.
- A book's mathematics should be intellectually and developmentally appropriate for its audience.
- A book should involve the reader in its mathematics.
- A book should provide readers the information needed to do its mathematics.
- A book's story and mathematics should complement each other.
- A book should facilitate readers' use, application, transfer, and generalization of its mathematics.
- The resources needed to help readers benefit from a book's mathematics should not be too great.

or mathematical definitions. On a more subtle level, the pictures, illustrations, diagrams, number lines, and such that a book's text refers to should actually present the referred-to material. To tell the reader that a father and daughter have 2 arms around a teddy bear's head and then present a picture on the facing page that shows only 1 arm around the teddy bear's head, as was done in *Ten, Nine, Eight* (Bang, 1983), is unacceptable. Similarly, to show a picture of "Grandma" coming into a room with a tray of 58 cookies that are to be divided among 12 children and then on the next page to show Grandma now in the room with the same tray containing 68 cookies, as is done in *The Doorbell Rang* (Hutchins, 1986), is simply inappropriate.

The mathematics in most children's books is correct, but there are enough books with incorrect mathematics for this to be of serious concern. To determine if a book's mathematics is correct and accurate it is necessary to evaluate to what extent a book's text, pictures, illustrations, diagrams, graphs, charts, numbers, equations, algorithms, and scale are accurate and correct, partially incorrect due to minor errors, or incorrect because of major errors. Typical examples of incorrect mathematics found in children's books follow.

In *One Was Johnny* (Sendak, 1962), Maurice Sendak shows the reader Johnny's room, into which 9 different creatures enter. The text for the first several pages of this counting book reads:

1 was Johnny who lived by himself
2 was a rat who jumped on his shelf

3 was a cat who chased the rat
4 was a dog who came in and sat

Here cardinal numbers are being used to depict the order in which either people or animals enter Johnny's room. Ordinal numbers should have been used instead of cardinal numbers and the mathematically correct text should read 1st, 2nd, 3rd, and 4th instead of 1, 2, 3, 4.

The difficulty created by confusing cardinal and ordinal numbers becomes increasingly apparent in the second half of *One Was Johnny* when each of the creatures that entered Johnny's room now leaves it. For example, the reader is told about the dog being the 6th creature to leave Johnny's room by Sendak's labeling it with the number 4. (This occurs because the dog was the 4th creature to enter the room.) Assigning cardinal numbers to items that are referred to in an ordinal context is mathematically incorrect and can create confusion for readers (Ballenger, Benham, & Hosticka, 1984).

FIGURE 4.2 Literary standards for evaluating children's mathematics books

---

Plot	A book's plot or story should be well developed and imaginative, flowing logically, believably, and sensibly from one idea to the next.
Characterization	A book's characters should be well portrayed and believable.
Style	A book should contain a vivid and interesting writing style that actively involves the child.
Language	A book should use correct grammar and punctuation and age-appropriate language and style.
Readability	A book's readability and knowledge content should be appropriate to the reader's age.
Interest	A book's interest level should be relevant and developmentally age-appropriate to the reader.
Enrichment	A book should enrich the child.
Graphics	A book's illustrations, pictures, or graphics should be well chosen, appealing, relevant to the text, and representative of a child's view of the world.
Unity	A book's plot, content, and graphics should convey the same stylistic message.
Respect	A book's tone should respect the reader, its characters should provide positive role models for readers, and its characters should be culturally diverse and free from stereotype.
Physical traits	A book should be visually appealing, well organized, durable, and laid out to produce easy comprehension.

Too Many Eggs (Butler, 1988), a book about a bear cooking, contains a statement that illustrates the incorrect use of mathematical terminology. The following is the sequence of statements on the third page of the book:

With a large wooden spoon,
Mrs. Bear mixed together lots of sugar,
loads of butter, some honey, and
a mass of flour in a huge bowl.
How much sugar?
How much butter?
How much honey?
How much flour?
I do not know.
Mrs. Bear never, never counts
anything properly, because—
Mrs. Bear cannot count!

Nor should she be counting these things! She should be measuring them! Text that confuses counting and measuring is simply incorrect.

The King's Chessboard (Birch, 1988) is based on the well-known anecdote of putting a grain of rice on one square of a chessboard, doubling that amount and placing it on the next square of the chessboard on the next day, and continuing this doubling activity for 64 days. It is about how the resulting numbers become very large very quickly. It presents an interesting example of arithmetic inaccuracy:

The Grand Superintendent said to himself, "Tomorrow there will be eight sacks—over half a ton! I must tell the King!"
But the King was away hunting in the mountains that day and the next. So on the following day the Grand Superintendent had to send the wise man over a ton of rice. The next day it was two tons. And still the King had not returned to the palace. There was nothing to be done. . . . The next day four tons. . . . Then eight tons. (p. 17)

The problem here is that when one successively doubles "over half a ton" four times, one might get anywhere from a little bit more than 8 tons to a little bit less than 16 tons (assuming that "over half a ton" means between half a ton and a ton). One would never get exactly the progression of 2 tons, 4 tons, and 8 tons. This book treats fractional amounts as though they do not make much of a difference in mathematics—but they can, of course, make a very large cumulative difference. In this and other sequences of text, *The King's Chessboard* presents children with the message that it is acceptable to be "sloppy" and inaccurate while doing mathematics.

A BOOK'S MATHEMATICS SHOULD BE EFFECTIVELY PRESENTED

In evaluating how effectively a book presents its mathematical ideas, a variety of issues must be considered, including the following:

Do the text, pictures, illustrations, diagrams, graphs, charts, numbers, equations, algorithms, and scale effectively present the book's mathematics?

Do the various components of the book (text, pictures, etc.) complement one another, have no effect on one another, or distract from one another's effectiveness?

If it is appropriate for the book to contain numbers, equations, diagrams, graphs, or other such items, are they present everywhere that is appropriate, only sometimes present, or altogether absent?

When mathematical ideas are introduced, are they accompanied by relevant examples (pictorial, graphic, concrete, etc.) designed to facilitate reader comprehension?

Does the book make the relationships among its mathematical ideas clear enough that there is a logical connection or "flow of meaning" from one idea to the next?

Overall, are the book's ideas clearly, effectively, and successfully presented; given a somewhat decent presentation; or poorly, unsatisfactorily, ambiguously, or unintelligibly presented? Examples of poorly presented mathematics in children's books abound.

In *Counting Wildflowers* (McMillan, 1986) the author presents the following items on page 4: the flower name of *wood lily*; photographs of 4 wood lilies, each containing 6 petals; the number 4; the word *four*; and a prominent drawing of 4 red circles and 6 green circles in a line. Is the reader supposed to observe 4 items (the 4 wood lilies), 6 items (the 6 petals in each wood lily), the pattern of 4×6 (the pattern of petals on the page), 10 items (the number of circles on the page), or the equation $4 + 6 = 10$ (the relation between red, green, and the total number of circles)? *I Can Count the Petals of a Flower* (Wahl & Wahl, 1976) avoids this confusion with the simplicity of its pages, each of which contains a color photograph of one flower, a simple line drawing of its petal structure, and a number (representing the number of petals it contains).

The Hare's Race (Baumann, 1976) provides an example of text that is poorly presented, particularly in relation to the illustration found on the same page. This is a book about a race between a hare and mole that parallels Aesop's fable about the hare and tortoise. One of the book's pages has an illustration of a mole having reached the 7-meter point of a 10-meter race track and contains the following text:

> But Hare didn't come.
> Four meters left, he thought.
> First I'll jump rope.
> He ran to the playground and jumped
> one-two-three-four-five-six-seven times.
> "Seven meters!" shouted Fox, Badger, and Crow.
> "Come on, Hare, come on!" (p. 15)

This confusing passage, and many others like it, leaves one wondering: How do the phrases "Four meters left," "First," "one-two-three-four-five-six-seven," and "Seven meters," and the illustration showing the mole at the 7-meter mark of the 10-meter race track all relate to each other. This represents an ineffective attempt to present one of the following mathematics facts: $10 - 6 = 4$, $10 - 7 + 1 = 4$, or $10 - 4 + 1 = 7$.

In *Anno's Mysterious Multiplying Jar* (Anno & Anno, 1983), the meaning of factorials is presented in a series of matched equations and diagrams of dot arrays, one set per page. (Factorial is a mathematical function. For any whole number N, "N!" is read "N factorial," and usually defined as N! $= N \times (N - 1)$!" In other words, "4!" is read "four factorial" and $4! = 4 \times 3!$ $= 4 \times 6$. A dot array is a rectangular arrangement of dots where the number of dots the rectangle is high and wide usually represent specific mathematical quantities, such as the first and second elements in the expression $3 \times 2!$.) *Anno's Mysterious Multiplying Jar* presents its matched equations and diagrams for the numbers from one to six as follows:

$1! = 1 \times 1! = 1$	is portrayed by a	*1*	by *1*	array of dots
$2! = 2 \times 1! = 2$	is portrayed by a	*1*	by *2*	array of dots
$3! = 3 \times 2! = 6$	is portrayed by a	*3*	by *2*	array of dots
$4! = 4 \times 3! = 24$	is portrayed by a	*6*	by *4*	array of dots
$5! = 5 \times 4! = 120$	is portrayed by a	*12*	by *10*	array of dots
$6! = 6 \times 5! = 720$	is portrayed by a	*30*	by *24*	array of dots

While these configurations accurately represent the quantities of dots involved, they fail to reflect the equations on which the progression is based; that is, 5! should have 5 rows of 24 dots (representing 4!), not 12 rows of 10 dots. In a book about the meaning of factorials, the diagrams should systematically present a "picture" of what is meant, as shown in Figure 4.3. Anno's diagrams fail to do this, both because there is no systematic development of horizontal versus vertical presentation of the dots in his dot arrays

Figure 4.3 Dot arrays

a 1 by 1 array	a 2 by 1 array	a 3 by 2 array	a 4 by 6 array
•	• • (2 by 1)	(3 by 2 dots)	(4 by 6 dots)

a 5 by 24 array

and because the horizontal and vertical dimensions of the arrays do not have a one-to-one correspondence to the equations they are designed to represent and give meaning to. Thus the mathematical ideas portrayed are not as effectively presented as possible.

Many books miss the chance to maximize the effectiveness of their presentation of mathematical ideas because they do not tactfully present numbers, equations, diagrams, graphs, or other such symbolic representations everywhere that is appropriate for them to appear. An example of this can be found in *Fat Cat* (Hales, Hales, & Amstutz, 1985), a story about a pirate captain and her 9 crew members who act out the 10 addition number family. One two-page spread, which illustrates 4 pirates on one page and 6 on the other, reads as follows:

> On silent paws,
> while the captain snores,
> three pirates wash the plates.
>
> Then before she wakes
> six make some cakes
> to feed her for her tea.
>> Four and six make ten.
>> 4 and 6 make 10 (pp. 9, 10)

Here mathematical equations are conspicuously absent. Why is *Fat Cat* missing the equation $4 + 6 = 10$, when it has pictures illustrating the equation, text illustrating the equation, and sentences paraphrasing the equation?

A final example of poorly presented mathematics involves many authors' hesitation to use precise mathematical language instead of a simplified form of colloquial English. For example, many authors avoid the word *equals* and substitute other, supposedly more familiar, words in its place, such as *make*. In *Fat Cat* (Hales et al., 1985) we discover that "Four and six make ten"; in *Richard Scarry's Best Counting Book Ever* (Scarry, 1975) we discover that 2 rabbits and 1 rabbit make 3 rabbits; while in *Bunches and Bunches of Bunnies* (Mathews, 1978) we discover that 4 times 4 "makes" 16. Can two numbers "build, assemble, construct, cause, create, invent, beget, or manufacture" another number? No, they cannot—not in any normal usage of the English language. If "four and six" were to "make" anything, they would probably make 46, not 10. There is nothing wrong with the word *equals*, or the symbol = either. Substituting other words for *equals* misses a chance to effectively present mathematics.

A BOOK'S MATHEMATICS
SHOULD BE WORTHY OF BEING LEARNED

A question that must be asked of every book is whether or not its mathematics is worthy of being learned. The question usually refers to four areas of concern:

Is the book's mathematics of significant, questionable, or little value within the field of mathematics?

Is the book's mathematics of significant, questionable, or little value within our culture and the jobs pursued by its work force?

Is the book's mathematics likely to be useful to, encountered by, or relevant to the targeted audience?

Is the book's mathematics likely to be interesting and enjoyable or to have little intrinsic value for its targeted audience?

These can be difficult questions to answer for several reasons: because they are based in value-laden inquiries to which there are not always easy answers; because what is considered to be significant within the field of professional mathematics is constantly changing as the field evolves; because what society considers to be useful, relevant, or of interest to children is constantly changing as society evolves; and because few evaluators of children's trade books feel comfortable making expert judgments about mathematics, society, and children.

Clearly, books that deal with topics such as counting, addition, and linear measurement contain mathematics that is worth learning. Some evaluators might have difficulty making decisions about books dealing with sets and fractals. Books that present the meaning of and how to do calculations with Roman numerals or an abacus may have been considered to contain mathematics worth learning during the first quarter of this century, but today they may be of relatively little value when compared with books that address the related mathematics of place value or computer programming. They might be considered of relatively little value both because of their lack of significance within the field of professional mathematics and our culture, and because of their lack of relevance and usefulness to children.

This standard does not exist to exclude all but "worthy" mathematical topics from children's books or to exclude books that do not include such "worthy" topics. It exists to point out that in evaluating children's books that contain mathematics, one must ask the question "Is the book's mathematics worthy of being learned?" If a mathematical topic is not deemed as worthy of having children's books written about it at a particular point in time, that does not necessarily mean that books should not be written about the topic. We must leave ourselves open to having children's books written about mathematical topics of historical interest and topics whose nature we are just beginning to explore.

A BOOK'S MATHEMATICS SHOULD BE VISIBLE
TO THE READER

When examining a book to determine if its mathematics will be visible to the reader, the central question asked is: Are all of the book's major mathematical ideas appropriately *highlighted* or are there *missed opportunities* to highlight mathematics? In evaluating a book to determine if its mathematics is optimally visible, only somewhat visible, or elusive to the reader, the following four concerns are focused on:

Are the book's mathematical ideas located everywhere that is appropriate for them to appear (text, illustrations, diagrams, equations, etc.) or are they missing from places where they belong?

To what extent will the book's mathematics be visible to the reader in its text, its pictures and illustrations, its diagrams and graphs, and its numbers, equations, and algorithms?

Is the book's mathematics highlighted in such a way that it is presented without distraction from surrounding details, or does the book address multiple topics simultaneously or include irrelevant and distracting information in a way that might disrupt the reader's understanding?

If mathematical ideas are simultaneously presented in text, illustrations, graphs, or other components of the book, will the reader notice the relationships among the different presentations?

After reading books to children, I have frequently found that while I have clearly seen the book's mathematics, the children to whom the book was read have missed the mathematics altogether—and this has occurred with teachers as well as children. For example, I remember discussing *The Doorbell Rang* (Hutchins, 1986) with a group of teachers, one of whom commented that she had read the book to her students for several years and never realized it contained mathematics, because the driving question of "what was going to happen next, when the doorbell rang?" diverted the readers' attention from everything else occurring in the book. Unfortunately, it is also the case that "Ma" said "I've made some cookies for tea" rather than "I've made 12 cookies for tea" and that not a single division equation is presented in the book, even though story lines and illustrations are clearly presented for the equations of $12 \div 2 = 6$, $12 \div 4 = 3$, $12 \div 6 = 2$, and $12 \div 12 = 1$. Why was the word *some* used instead of the word *twelve* or the numeral *12*, and why wasn't something tactfully inserted into the text or illustrations to help make the inherent mathematics visible?

The number of missed opportunities to highlight mathematics pictorially is surprising, particularly given the ease with which mathematics can be elegantly inserted into illustrations. A prime example of this can be found in books that present the counting song "Roll Over." The first round of the song is

10 in the bed and the little one said:
"Roll over! Roll over!"
They all rolled over and 1 fell out.

In succeeding rounds the number 10 is decreased to 9, 8, 7, and so on down to 1. The song can be viewed as either a "counting down by 1" activity, a "subtraction of 1" activity, or both. If it were conceived of as a "counting down by 1" activity, might it not be appropriate to present some form of a modified number line (or some other such device) so that children reading books that present the song could see where they were in the count from 10 to 1 and how each number relates to the others? If it were conceived of as a "subtraction by 1" activity, might it not be appropriate to present the subtraction equation (or some other such device) that corresponds to each round of the song?

In *Roll Over! A Counting Song* (Peek, 1981), two facing pages are devoted to each round of the song? In *Roll Over!* (Gerstein, 1984), the equivalent of three pages is devoted to each round of the song. The pages of both books contain ample room to unobtrusively insert something like a modified number line or a subtraction equation. Neither is presented, and the books miss their chance to highlight mathematics. This is particularly unfortunate for *Roll Over!*, since the footboard of the bed portrayed on each page contains a space where the subtraction equations could be written and because the 10 spokes out of which the footboard is constructed could easily have formed a number line.

Six Brave Explorers (Moerbeek & Dijs, 1988) illustrates how distracting text and graphics can obscure a book's major mathematical ideas and disrupt a reader's understanding of them. In this book about subtracting 1 from selected numbers, each two-page spread has a pop-up animal in the center that dominates the pages as well as text and illustrations that tell a subtraction story. For example, the page depicting "$4 - 1 = 3$" has the following components: In the middle of the two-page spread there is a pop-up panther; on the left-hand page there is the text "Four thirsty explorers taking time for tea" and an illustration of 4 explorers; and on the right-hand page there is the text "One poured for a panther—and then there were three" and an illustration of 1 explorer being carried by an Egyptian and 3 explorers walking. Here the mathematics is invisible to many children for several reasons: (1) There are too many different things occurring on the pages and they are dominated by a pop-up panther; (2) a "take-away" concept of subtraction is presented in the text that is not mirrored by the "subset" concept of subtraction that is presented in the illustrations; (3) the position of the 1 explorer who is being carried is adjacent to the 3 who are walking; and (4) there is no subtraction equation on the page.

The King's Chessboard (Birch, 1988) shows how mathematics can be hidden in an illustration in such a way as to be virtually invisible to the reader. The book is about how the powers of 2 grow to be very large very quickly, but it contains only one mathematical table showing the powers of 2. This table is written in a curved fashion across the ceiling of a house in which the main feature is a man using a scale to weigh rice. Here the powerful message that could be delivered by a mathematical table to reinforce the information presented in the book's text is lost because (1) the table is almost invisible within a complex illustration that presents many other items, and (2) even if readers noticed the table on the house's ceiling, they would probably not know how it relates to the numbers generated in the text because the numbers in the table are spread out over many pages in the book, and because the unit of measure keeps changing during the story (from grains to ounces to bags to sacks to tons of rice). *A Grain of Rice* (Pittman, 1986) is a slightly different version of the same story that does not present a single table or graph of the powers of 2.

The point is not to insist that mathematics must dominate and clutter the pages of children's books but to stress that if we wish children to benefit from a book's mathematics, then it must be visible to them as well as to adults.

A BOOK SHOULD PRESENT AN APPROPRIATE VIEW
OF MATHEMATICS

Every book presents a view of its contents. Mathematics can be presented as a boring, tedious, and dull subject that deals only with calculation or as an exciting problem-solving activity that is relevant to our everyday lives. The 10 specific criteria in Figure 4.4 reflect one interpretation of an appropriate view of mathematics. They also present an example of the types of specific criteria that give concrete meaning to each of the more general standards and make it possible to assess a book with respect to them.

FIGURE 4.4 **Specific criteria for the standard:**
"A book should present an appropriate view of mathematics"

A.1	Is mathematics portrayed as enjoyable, neutral, or distasteful?
A.2	Is mathematics portrayed as useful, simply existing, or of little practical everyday use?
A.3	Is mathematics portrayed as a subject that one uses with understanding and purpose or simply as an activity that one does?
A.4	Is mathematics portrayed as both a social and individual activity or solely as an individual activity?
A.5	Is mathematics portrayed as a creative problem-solving activity incorporating logic and reason or as an activity during which a single correct answer is sought by doing such things as counting, calculating, measuring, or graphing?
A.6	Is mathematics portrayed as involving active participation or passive observation?
A.7	Is mathematics portrayed as interrelated information, facts, concepts, skills, strategies, and procedures that relate to other fields of study and the real world or as a collection of isolated facts, skills, and so forth?
A.8	Is mathematics portrayed as an activity in which people use both their intellect and everyday objects—such as fingers, pencils, diagrams, embodiments, graphs, calculators, computers, and so forth—or as only an intellectual endeavor?
A.9	Is mathematics portrayed as accessible to all people—independent of gender, race, intelligence, cultural background, physical handicap, age, and so forth—or as something accessible to an "elite few"?
A10	Is mathematics portrayed as a language useful in formulating, clarifying, and communicating ideas to others and oneself through spoken and written media, or simply as an activity that yields answers to problems?

Books abound that represent good and poor examples of each of these criteria. Two books on telling time—*Time to . . .* (McMillan, 1989) and *When I Learn to Tell Time* (Johnson, 1990)—will be evaluated with respect to the 10 specific criteria in Figure 4.4, both to show how specific criteria can be used to evaluate books with respect to a standard and to provide meaning to the standard and its criteria.

Time to . . . contains 15 two-page spreads depicting events that occur hourly between 7:00 A.M. and 9:00 P.M. One page contains a vibrant color photograph of a boy engaged in an activity on its top four-fifths, with the words "TIME TO . . . " on the bottom left and a one- to five-word description of the activity on the bottom right. The facing page contains a photograph of a clock on the boy's bedroom wall on its top four-fifths, the time displayed digitally (7:00 A.M.) on its bottom left, and the time of day spelled out on the bottom right (as in "SEVEN O'CLOCK IN THE MORNING"). The activities include: wake up, eat breakfast, go to school, paint a picture, play at recess, eat lunch, swing, eat dinner, and fall asleep.

Time to . . . has beautiful photographs that are relevant to events in most children's lives and has three different representations of time: clock-face, digital display, and words (see Figure 4.5). However, it does not tell a story that is personally engaging to children or that shows children using time in any way.

When I Learn to Tell Time contains seven two-page spreads depicting events that occur in the life of a girl and her cat. They include rising at 7:00 A.M., sending her brother to school at 8:00 A.M., preparing lunch for grandma at 1:00 P.M., preparing to watch her favorite TV show at 3:00 P.M., and selecting a bedtime story to read at 7:00 P.M. Each two-page spread has three parts: The top four-fifths contains from three to eight color illustrations of the girl and cat engaging in an activity, the bottom one-fifth contains words that describe how telling time will give the girl the power to accomplish the illustrated activity, and the bottom right corner contains a clock-face with its time (e.g., "8 o'clock") written underneath (see Figure 4.6). The multiple illustrations on each page, most of which contain a clock with a slightly later time than in the previous illustration on that page, show time progressing toward an hour and by doing so tell the page's story.

When I Learn to Tell Time, by portraying a girl doing things that she could only do if she can tell time, shows how she gains power over her world and influence over others because of this ability. The book's warm, friendly, and humorous color illustrations are relevant to events in most children's lives and give the reader a vivid picture of its main actors. The girl and cat are portrayed wearing, watching, holding, carrying, and pointing to clocks or watches on every page of the book. The lack of a strong plot, however, detracts from the book's effectiveness, as does the heavy paperboard out of which it is constructed.

FIGURE 4.5 Pages 12–13 of *Time to . . .*

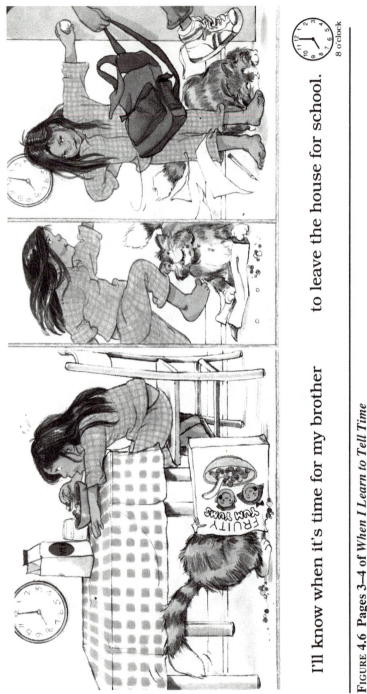

I'll know when it's time for my brother   to leave the house for school.

8 o'clock

FIGURE 4.6 Pages 3–4 of *When I Learn to Tell Time*

To determine how adequately each book presents an "appropriate view of mathematics," the books will be assessed on a scale of 1 to 5, where a positive ranking is designated by a 5, a neutral ranking by a 3, and a negative ranking by a 1. Each criterion and its application to the books under review will now be discussed. Table 4.1 is provided for ease in following the discussion. *Note that these assessments are relevant only to the standard under discussion, and assessment with respect to one standard cannot be assumed to be an overall assessment of a book.*

A.1: *Is mathematics portrayed as enjoyable, neutral, or distasteful? When I Learn to Tell Time* is rated 5 because the girl is shown enjoying her use of clocks and because being able to tell time allows her to do things she enjoys, such as watching her favorite TV show. In *Time to . . .* nobody uses mathematics; it is used solely to label when activities occur. As such, mathematics is portrayed as neither enjoyable nor distasteful, so it is given a neutral rating of 3.

A.2: *Is mathematics portrayed as useful, simply existing, or of little practical everyday use? When I Learn to Tell Time* shows how a girl gains power over her everyday world and influence over others because of her ability to tell time. It shows how this ability is a useful skill that allows one to actively participate in controlling one's destiny and to get what one desires from life. It is rated 5. In *Time to . . .* the boy's life is portrayed as totally regulated by clock time, yet none of its characters use time-telling devices, look at clocks, or show any awareness of what time it is. Time exists in their lives and governs their activities, but they do not use time. They are not users of mathematics, but simply creatures caught in a world it can describe. It is rated 2, because the boy's bedroom has a clock in it.

A.3: *Is mathematics portrayed as a subject that one uses with understanding and purpose or simply as an activity that one does? When I Learn to Tell Time* shows a girl using a watch with understanding and purpose to accomplish personal goals. It is rated 5. In *Time to . . .* none of the main characters engage in mathematical activity, let alone engage in mathematics with either understanding or purpose. Time, and thus mathematics, is portrayed as simply calibrating the world in

TABLE 4.1 Rating of time books

Book	A.1	A.2	A.3	A.4	A.5	A.6	A.7	A.8	A.9	A.10	SUM
When I Learn To Tell Time	5	5	5	5	3	5	5	5	4	4	46
Time To...	3	2	1	1	1	1	3	3	4	2	21

which things exist: It is external to the lives of the characters. In addition, this book does not ask the reader to do mathematics with understanding and purpose but simply to observe how clock time can label activities. It is rated 1.

A.4: *Is mathematics portrayed as both a social and individual activity or solely as an individual activity? When I Learn to Tell Time* portrays a girl, her cat, and other members of her family interacting over time issues. For example, the cat points to a clock when it gets hungry and the girl helps her brother and father get to school and work on time. What is critical here is that the characters talk to each other about mathematical ideas, not simply that they talk to each other. It is rated 5. In *Time to . . .* nobody engages in mathematical activity, let alone engaging in it socially. It is rated 1.

A.5: *Is mathematics portrayed as a creative problem-solving activity incorporating logic and reason or as an activity during which a single correct answer is sought by doing such things as counting, calculating, measuring, or graphing?* The characters in *When I Learn to Tell Time* encounter the problem of making sure events occur at certain times during the day. These are real problems, but hardly ones that involve much creative problem solving in which logic and reason are critically used. It is rated 3. The characters in *Time to . . .* encounter no mathematical problems. It is rated 1.

A.6: *Is mathematics portrayed as involving active participation or passive observation? When I Learn to Tell Time* is rated 5 because the main characters are quite actively involved with telling time in such a way that the reader is lured into actively reading the book's clocks along with them. *Time to . . .* is rated 1 because the reader is a passive observer to the time-telling activity and the main characters are not actively engaged in any mathematical activity.

A.7: *Is mathematics portrayed as interrelated information, facts, concepts, skills, strategies, and procedures that relate to other fields of study and the real world or as a collection of isolated facts, skills, and so forth?* Both books show time as connected with children's everyday world. *When I Learn to Tell Time* is rated 5 because the girl and her cat see the relationship of time to their everyday lives and communicate such to the reader. *Time to . . .* is rated 3 because the story's narration and the configuration of clock, text, and illustrations on each page show the reader how time is interconnected with the lives of the book's characters, even though those characters are not shown as having awareness of time concepts.

A.8: *Is mathematics portrayed as an activity in which people use both their intellect and everyday objects—such as fingers, pencils, diagrams, em-*

bodiments, graphs, calculators, computers, and so forth—or as only an intellectual endeavor? This criterion determines whether a book supports the stereotype of mathematics as an abstract intellectual endeavor or presents a more realistic picture of children using their intellects as well as everyday materials to do mathematics. *When I Learn to Tell Time* is rated 5 because the girl and her cat constantly use clocks to get what they want. In *Time to . . .* the reader is shown the clock in the boy's bedroom with each illustration, and it is made clear that clocks relate to doing mathematics. However, the boy is not shown using clocks or watches, and in fact there is never even a clock or watch included in a photograph in which he appears. *Time to . . .* is therefore rated 3.

A.9:   *Is mathematics portrayed as accessible to all people—independent of gender, race, intelligence, cultural background, physical handicap, age, and so forth—or as something accessible to an "elite few"?* This criterion determines whether a book presents the stereotype that only "brainy" people (mostly white middle-class males) like or are good at mathematics. Because *When I Learn to Tell Time* is about a girl doing mathematics and thus counteracts the stereotype that girls are not good at mathematics, it is rated 4. *Time to . . .* is rated 4 because it includes several minorities in its photographs; unfortunately, none are portrayed doing mathematics.

A.10: *Is mathematics portrayed as a language useful in formulating, clarifying, and communicating ideas to others and oneself through spoken and written media, or simply as an activity that yields answers to problems?* Neither book is rich in dialogue about powerful mathematical ideas. However, *When I Learn to Tell Time* has the girl and cat nonverbally communicating needs and desires to each other that are related to the time of day. As such, it is rated 4. *Time to . . .* is rated 2 because its characters do not use language to communicate any mathematical ideas and because when the book does "talk" to the reader, it answers by rote the simple question, "What time is it now?"

Several points emerge from the discussion of this standard. First, it is difficult to comprehend the meaning of the standard "A book should present an appropriate view of mathematics" in and of itself. Specific criteria that are more concretely defined give meaning to the more general standard. Second, it is more difficult to rate a book as excellent, mediocre, or poor according to this general standard than to rate it on each of the specific criteria because they concretely focus attention on a single area of concern. Third, it is possible to differentiate between books and rate them. With its rating of 46 out of a possible 50 points, *When I Learn to Tell Time* would be considered to present a far more appropriate view of mathematics than *Time to . . .*, with its rating of 21. Fourth, *reasons can be given for why the books are rated the way they are.* One does not need to just "intuitively feel" that a book should have a high or low rating. Fifth, these reasons can go beyond the surface characteristics of a book (such as whether or not a book's main characters wear watches) to examine hidden messages (such as whether or not mathematics is portrayed as giving characters control over their world). Sixth, it is easier to rate a book when one has several books on a similar topic to compare it with than when one must rate it out of context. In summary, the standards and their defining criteria allow one to make a more insightful and reasoned decision about whether or not a book is excellent, mediocre, or poor than one could make without them.

It must be noted that evaluation of children's mathematics trade books is tied to what society considers to be both "good mathematics" and "good children's literature," both of which opinions evolve over time. *Socrates and the Three Little Pigs* (Anno, 1986) is an excellent example of a work that, only within the last few decades, would be rated poorly on the criterion (A.9) of whether a book portrays mathematics "as accessible to all people. . . ." In the book, which is about combinatorial analysis, Socrates (who is a male wolf) is portrayed as a philosopher who spends most of his time thinking while his wife Xanthippe is portrayed as a extremely fat woman who does not at all like to think and is primarily concerned with when she is going to eat. Here the reader learns that both sexes are not equally capable of doing mathematics, a view that is no longer deemed appropriate or accurate, although it may not have bothered people a few decades ago. Similar issues related to multicultural perspectives must be sensitively dealt with, particularly when issues of "Who gets to decide what is or is not appropriate?" are raised (Whitin & Wilde, 1995).

A BOOK'S MATHEMATICS SHOULD BE INTELLECTUALLY AND DEVELOPMENTALLY APPROPRIATE FOR ITS AUDIENCE

Almost everyone who writes about evaluating children's mathematics trade books asserts that it is important for such books to be "developmentally appropriate" for their targeted audience, that is, the range of ages or grade levels of children for whom the book is intended. Unfortunately, we are never told how to actually determine what a book's intended audience is, what is actually meant by the phrase *developmentally appropriate*, or how to determine the level of sophistication and difficulty of a mathematics topic.

The following variables help one determine the appropriateness of a book for a child of a certain age: its reading level (if the child is to read the book);

the conceptual level of the language; the interest level of the story; the interest level of the illustrations; the grade level at which the book's concepts are introduced in the school curriculum; the grade level at which the book's concepts are fully developed (and henceforth maintained) in the school curriculum; the developmental level at which the book presents its ideas (preoperational, concrete operational, or formal operational); and the symbolic level at which the book's ideas are presented (concrete, pictorial, diagrammatic, symbolic, etc.). Examining the grade levels (or ages) at which these variables cluster—if they do cluster, and they sometimes do not—tells a great deal about what an appropriate audience is for a book. Unfortunately, actually determining the value of all of these variables is not easy.

In addition, determining a book's targeted audience is only part of the task. One must also determine if the level of difficulty and sophistication at which the book's mathematics is presented matches that of the book's targeted audience. In order to determine if a book's mathematics is intellectually and developmentally appropriate, somewhat appropriate, or inappropriate for its targeted audience, we must answer questions such as the following:

> To what extent is the intellectual level of the book's mathematics the same as or different from its reading level, the conceptual level of its language, the interest level of its story, the interest level of its illustrations, the mathematics achievement level of its audience, the developmental level of its intended audience, the symbolic level at which its ideas are presented, and the grade level at which that mathematics is introduced by the school curriculum?
>
> Are the book's mathematical ideas and activities at a consistent level of intellectual difficulty or at variable levels of difficulty?
>
> Are new mathematics concepts related to or not related to children's prior knowledge and experience?
>
> Will the pacing with which new mathematics concepts are introduced be appropriate or overwhelming to the intended readers?
>
> Is the book's mathematical information density (number of ideas per paragraph, page, or chapter) appropriate or inappropriate for the target age group?
>
> Could the book's mathematics, in the context of its story, be enjoyed beyond the targeted age group or is it limited to the targeted age group?

Although the mathematics in most children's books is *presented* in a way that is intellectually and developmentally appropriate for targeted audiences, many books contain mathematics *concepts* that are intellectually and developmentally inappropriate for those audiences.

How Much Is a Million? (Schwartz, 1985) is an example of one such book. One version of it is published in Big Book format, which would indicate that it is appropriate for children in kindergarten, first grade, or second grade. Educational material supply houses have recommended it for grades K–3 (NASCO, 1995; Cuisenaire Company of America, 1991), and the book's illustrations and text (all capitals) target it for those grades. However, *How Much Is a Million?* deals with the relationship between the sizes of a million, a billion, and a trillion. Are most children in these grades ready to deal with numbers this large? Not according to most mathematics educators. Even if second graders were capable of dealing with a number the size of a million, are they capable of understanding the difference in size between a million, a billion, and a trillion? Mathematics textbooks do not introduce such topics at this grade level. When the author speaks about the arithmetic in *How Much Is a Million?* at the back of the book, he speaks about such calculations as dividing 4 billion feet by 5,280 feet per mile. Are most third graders ready to deal with this problem, let alone children in grades K–2? Not according to most school curricula. The problem with *How Much Is a Million?* is that the level of its mathematics is different from its reading level, the conceptual level of its language, the interest level of its story, and the interest level of its illustrations. The book can be read to children and they can enjoy its story, but they will be too young to fully understand its mathematics.

From a different perspective, *Richard Scarry's Best Counting Book Ever* (Scarry, 1975) is typical of a variety of counting books that seem to be designed to help children learn to count—and learn the meaning of the counting numbers—from 1 to 10. However, after carefully introducing the numbers from 1 to 10, the book extends the number of objects counted first to 20 (where the number of objects counted is incremented by 1 on each succeeding page) and then to 100 (where the number of objects counted is incremented by 10 and grouped in clusters of 5—40 = 5 × 8—on each succeeding page). What must be focused on here is the difficulty of meaningfully counting from 1 to 10, as compared to meaningfully counting from 1 to 100, as compared to meaningfully counting from 1 to 100 by 10s in groups of 5. The issue here is: Are the book's mathematical ideas and activities at a consistent level of intellectual difficulty or at variable levels of difficulty? Here there is a mixing of (what might be approximated to be) kindergarten tasks with second-grade tasks.

A BOOK SHOULD INVOLVE THE READER
IN ITS MATHEMATICS

When evaluating how involved a child might get with a book's mathematics, at least three factors need consideration: the degree to which a book stimulates different interactive modalities, the participatory level at which the child becomes involved with the book's mathematics, and the extent to which the book's story and illustrations stimulate interest in its mathematics. Note that the concern here is with how involved the child is likely to become with the book's mathematics, not its story.

There are at least three different ways that children can become involved with a book's mathematics—becoming intellectually involved in thinking about the mathematics, physically involved in doing the mathematics, and emotionally involved with the impact that the book's mathematics have on its characters or on the child's own life. For each of these interactive modalities, one must attempt to determine the degree of involvement that is likely to result when a child reads a book. One must also determine whether that involvement will result in meaningful interactions. For example, because a book contains physical manipulatives to use when reading it does not necessarily mean that these manipulatives will encourage meaningful involvement with its mathematics. The clock whose hands the reader must set to the specified hour in *What Time Is Grandma Coming?* (Seymour, 1983) and the mirror the reader uses on the pages of *The Mirror Puzzle Book* (Walter, 1985) to learn about symmetry result in high levels of meaningful involvement. However, the eggs that must be arranged in *Too Many Eggs* (Butler, 1988) and the beads that must be moved on the counting abacus in *Albert Moves In* (Kubler, 1988) are likely to provide the reader with a low level of meaningful mathematical involvement and a high level of frustration because the books contain inadequate instructions for the use of their associated manipulatives.

Three different participatory levels at which children's books engage their readers have been identified, and knowing the level at which a book engages a child tells a great deal about how involved a child is likely to become with its mathematics:

Level 1: The reader observes the results of mathematical endeavors without being told how the mathematics is done.
Level 2: The reader "listens in" to a character's or the author's thought processes while mathematics is being done, in such a way that the reader is shown how to do the mathematics; however, the reader is not required to do the mathematics in order to understand or appreciate the book.
Level 3: The reader is required to do mathematics in the book in order to meaningfully read and understand it.

At level 1 we find books such as *Inch by Inch* (Lionni, 1960) and *How Much Is a Million?* (Schwartz, 1985). In *How Much Is a Million?* the reader discovers that "If you wanted to count from one to one million . . . it would take you about 23 days" (p. 4). The reader, however, is not expected to do either the counting or the calculations that lead to this conclusion. In *Inch by Inch* the reader listens to the result of an inchworm measuring objects, but the reader does not measure and, in fact, does not even see how the inchworm measures. One only sees a picture of an inchworm making the shape of a mountain fold on the back of the robin and hears it counting out "One, two, three, four, five inches." (Note that if the robin's tail is measured with a ruler, it is not 5 inches, as stated in the book.)

At level 2 we find books such as *Ed Emberley's Little Drawing Book of the Farm* (Emberley, 1973) and *One More Thing, Dad* (Thompson, 1980), where the reader "listens in" on the thought processes involved in a mathematical endeavor and is thus shown how to do the mathematics, but is never required to do it in order to understand or appreciate the book. In *Ed Emberley's Little Drawing Book of the Farm*, the reader is carefully shown how to draw animals (such as a dog, cat, or pig) by sequentially and cumulatively adding shapes (such as a square, circle, triangle, or squiggle) to one another through a 10-step sequence of drawings. Here we see Emberley's mathematical thought processes and can appreciate them without having to engage in them ourselves. In the counting book *One More Thing, Dad*, a child, Caleb, collects objects (such as a sandwich, an orange, and a blanket) to take on a picnic while the reader listens to him and watches him count on his fingers to keep track of how many objects he is bringing with him. Here the coordinated illustrations and text let readers actually see Caleb engaging in the counting process without having to do so themselves. This is quite different from most counting books, where we only see a number word or numeral on a page that is associated with the corresponding number of objects.

At level 3 the reader is required to do mathematics in order to meaningfully read the book and understand it. In doing so the reader might do the mathematics either adjacent to the book (for example, with paper and pencil) or by interacting with the book (for example, counting objects within it or using a mirror on it). Here we find books such as *Make a Bigger Puddle, Make a Smaller Worm* (Walter, 1971) and *Count with Little Bunny* (Ziefert & Ernst, 1988). In *Make a Bigger Puddle, Make a Smaller Worm*, the reader must use a mirror on the pages of the book in order to "see" the book's meaning (geometrical concepts related to symmetry). For example, the reader is presented with a picture of 1 sailboat in a lake and asked to make 2 boats that are far apart, or shown a picture of a plate with about a third of it broken off and asked to fix the plate. Here the use of the mirror (to do mathematics) on the pages of the book is necessary in order to read (see) the book's meaning. *Count with Little Bunny* is a counting book in which the reader is required to take plastic "colorform" stickers off a bookshelf on the last two pages of the book and place them on other pages of the book according to instructions. For example, on a page depicting Little Bunny next to a slide in a garden, the reader is told: "Little Bunny wants to play with cars. Give her four cars. . . . If you give her one more, then she'll have five." Here, in order to complete a page in the book, the reader must first get four car stickers from the bookshelf and place them on the slide or in the garden and then get one more car sticker from the bookshelf and place it on the page with the others. The reader "does" the mathematics rather than just "reading about" the mathematics.

The extent to which a child gets involved with a book's mathematics is significantly influenced by his or her interest in the book's story and illustrations. A good story and illustrations facilitate a child's involvement with a book's mathematics—when that mathematics is appropriately highlighted—while a poor story and illustrations inhibit involvement. When a high-interest story and illustrations are combined with higher participatory levels, the reader is more likely to actually "do" a book's mathematics than when lower levels of such exist.

A BOOK SHOULD PROVIDE READERS THE INFORMATION NEEDED TO DO ITS MATHEMATICS

Books that ask readers to do mathematics must be examined with respect to whether they provide the reader with the support necessary to complete the mathematical tasks. This involves determining whether the following things are provided for the reader:

Sufficiently clear instructions about how to complete the book's mathematical tasks

Any information that is needed to complete the mathematical tasks

Any physical materials needed to complete the task (are they either provided in the book or easily accessible?)

A means of determining if answers obtained to problems posed in the book are correct

It should be noted that not all books *require* the reader to do mathematics while reading them; a reader might be asked to do a book's mathematics either to enjoy the book more or to understand its events better.

Many of Anno's books ask children to do mathematics. Some contain instructions that clearly inform the reader how to complete their mathematical tasks, but the instructions in others leave the reader wondering what is to be done. In *Anno's Math Games* (Anno, 1987) and *Anno's Math Games II* (Anno,

1989), the instructions are clear and the tasks can be performed without difficulty. These books carefully lead the reader through the tasks in the company of two elves, Kriss and Kross, frequently showing the reader how to do sample problems before asking the reader to do similar ones. In *Anno's Counting House* (Anno, 1982), the instructions could not be read by a child who was just learning to count and if they were read to a child by an adult, the child would not be able to understand them. For a child to fully benefit from the book, a mathematically sophisticated adult would have to read the instructions in the front of the book several times, carefully explore the relationships between its instructions and contents, acquire the physical manipulatives the book suggests one use while reading it, and then carefully explain to a child the nature of the problem to be solved. The book was recently given to two mathematically sophisticated teachers who were asked to read it and explain what children could learn from it. The teachers, who had taught various grade levels from kindergarten to college mathematics, found the task difficult to complete until they had discussed the book. *Anno's Counting House* is a book in which the problem to be solved and the instructions that describe that problem are not clear until after the problem has been solved.

Albert Moves In (Kubler, 1988) provides an example of a book with inadequate instructions on how to complete its mathematical tasks. What is called a bead abacus is built into the book to help the reader keep track of the number of items that Albert brings with him as he moves into a new house. The difficulty is that it is not clear what the reader is to do with the bead abacus. For example, on the book's first two (facing) pages, the reader sees a picture of Albert taking 1 bike and 2 balls from a truck, reads text stating that Albert brought 1 bike and 2 balls, and encounters an "abacus" containing 10 beads that can be moved from one side of the "abacus" to the other. What is one to do? Should one first move 1 bead on the abacus and then 2 beads to show the result of bringing $1 + 2 = 3$ objects? Or should one move 1 bead to represent the count of "one," then move that bead back so that 2 beads can be moved to represent the count of "two"? The former seems to be the natural thing to do until one progresses in the book and runs out of beads. Having misinterpreted what the beads are to be used for, what does one now do? Does one engage in the second task mentioned above or simply decide that the book's mathematics and manipulatives do not complement each other or make much sense when used together?

Although *The Pushcart War* (Merrill, 1964) provides an example of a delightful book that is full of mathematics, it does not provide the reader with the information needed to complete its (frequently hidden) mathematical tasks. Unfortunately, the reader who does not think about the book's mathematics will miss much of the book's humor and not fully appreciate its plot. Two examples illustrate this. The reader should realize that this book, which is a history of a war between pushcart peddlers and truck drivers in New York in 1986, was copyrighted in MCMLXIV (yes, it was copyrighted in 1964, 22 years prior to its supposed occurrence, and the copyright is presented only in the form of a Roman numeral). The reader should also be able to determine the volume of a ton of peas in order to see how difficult it would be to hide them in a small shop, which was searched by police who could not find them. (The peas were used as part of a weapon to destroy truck tires.) *The Pushcart War* does not provide the reader the necessary information to solve this problem. In both of these examples readers are likely to overlook mathematics problems that give insight into the book and its humor.

Many books require a reader to use physical materials in order to complete their mathematics. The ease with which the materials can be obtained affects the ease with which the book's mathematics can be completed. Materials can be provided with the book, can be easily accessible, or can be difficult to obtain. *How High Is Pepperoni?* (Planet Dexter, 1995), which requires the use of a measuring tape to solve its problems related to length measurement, provides a measuring tape with the book. *What Is Symmetry?* (Sitomer & Sitomer, 1970) requires the use of easily found household items such as paper, pencil, and scissors to solve problems related to symmetry. *The M&M's Counting Book* (McGrath, 1994) requires the use of M&M's, which can be easily purchased, to help children explore counting, addition, subtraction, and geometric shapes. To explore the mathematics of *The Pushcart War*, it would be necessary to have materials, such as large quantities of pins and peas, that would take considerable time to obtain, count, and measure.

A book can take many approaches to helping a reader determine whether answers obtained to problems posed are correct. It can provide the reader with the solution, a set of hints, a self-correcting device, or a suggestion of how to find the solution elsewhere. It can also require the reader to ask someone else (friend, parent, or teacher) whether the solution is correct. Sometimes it is not possible for the reader to verify a solution (other than through his or her own insights into the problem and the solution obtained). *Anno's Hat Tricks* (Nozaki & Anno, 1985) makes the reader an actor in the book—called Shadowchild, whose shadow is depicted on most of the pages of the story—and then proceeds to carry out a discussion with the reader during which logic problems are posed, methods of solution are discussed, and solutions are provided as part of the book's story (frequently a page or two after they are posed). *Make a Bigger Puddle, Make a Smaller Worm* (Walter, 1971) poses problems requiring the use of a mirror on its pages (for example, to make a broken plate whole, as mentioned toward the end of the previous section). The mirror acts as a self-correcting device, with the reader being able to "see" the solution to the book's "problems" by looking in the mirror on the book's pages. In *Sideways Arithmetic from Wayside School* (Sachar, 1989) problems are posed, hints are given, and solutions are found in the back of the book. Other books, such as *The Pushcart War* (Merrill, 1964), neither formally highlight the problems posed nor provide solutions.

A BOOK'S STORY AND MATHEMATICS
SHOULD COMPLEMENT EACH OTHER

To determine how well a book's story and mathematics complement each other, it is necessary to evaluate the extent to which the mathematical issues arise naturally out of the plot, the mathematics adds to the story, the story is sufficiently interesting to support the mathematics, and the presentation of the mathematics supports or interferes with the narrative and illustrative style. It should then be possible to determine whether the book's story and mathematics are complementary, have no effect on each other, or detract from each other.

Four books that deal with the mathematics of world standard time zones illustrate different ways a book's story and mathematics can affect each other. Standard time zones can be approached from different perspectives: the science underlying them (rotation of the Earth), the mathematics underlying them (division of the Earth into 360 degrees of longitude with a 24-hour day gives 24 zones covering 15 degrees of longitude each), the social consequences of their existence (it is not the same time of day everywhere on the Earth at the same instant), their history (they were established in 1884), and the social problems that caused their establishment (the difficulties of using railroad timetables in the mid-1800s when traveling between cities whose local time was based on sun time).

This Book Is About Time (Burns, 1978) spends 13 pages discussing standard time zones from the perspectives of their mathematics, social consequences, history, and the social problems that led to their establishment. The author presents a connected series of personal stories describing the social problems that were resolved by the establishment of world times zones based on a mathematical model. The book is rich in its conversational style, has cartoons of people dealing with mathematical problems, and has experiments that the reader can engage in. The discussion of time zones is interesting because it is the story of people confronting problems that have mathematical solutions. The mathematics arises naturally out of the story, and the story and mathematics complement each other.

Time in Your Life (Adler, 1955) spends 6 pages discussing standard time zones from the perspectives of their mathematics, social consequences, and history. The discussion (which is not rich enough to be a cohesive story) consists of bland encyclopedic generalizations into which mathematical information is inserted—specifics about time zones that answer questions of where (in terms of longitude) and when (in terms of world standard clock time) but never address issues of why. Rather than complementing each other, the book's mathematics and story merely coexist: The mathematics detracts from the "story," and the "story" is too weak to give vitality to the mathematics.

All in a Day (Anno et al., 1986) contains 16 pages of text and beautiful color illustrations showing that it is not the same time of day everywhere in the world at the same instant. The story is dominated by 72 illustrations, each of which shows a typical activity engaged in by a child at a particular time of day in a different part of the world and is labeled with a location, date, and time. This beautiful book eloquently depicts the existence of and effect of time zones on people's lives (this is its mathematical message). However, its story—about a shipwrecked boy—is so weak that it gets lost among the illustrations that convey its mathematical message. Here the mathematics of the book comes across as being genuine, but the story comes across as being contrived simply as a way to present the labeled illustrations that convey the mathematics. As such, the mathematics overwhelms the story and detracts from it.

Anno's Sundial (Anno, 1985) is a 28-page picture book containing 13 pop-up sundials, many of which can actually be used to tell time. The mathematics of time zones (the mathematics of longitude and latitude and how they relate to sun time) is eloquently presented in the book's discussion of the use and construction of sundials. Here the story and mathematics of sundials so completely complement each other that they cannot be disentangled: Without the mathematics there would be no story, and without the story there would be no mathematics.

These books illustrate four ways in which a book's story and mathematics can relate to each other: the mathematics can grow out of the story (as in *This Book Is About Time*); they can be completely integrated (as in *Anno's Sundial*); they can detract from each other by coexisting in noncomplementary ways (as in *Time in Your Life*); or either the story or mathematics can overwhelm the other (as in *All in a Day*).

Many other examples exist of how books' mathematics and stories relate. For example, *Six Foolish Fisherman* (Elkin, 1957) (about six fishermen who think one is missing because the counter never includes himself when counting) and *Alexander, Who Used to Be Rich Last Sunday* (Viorst, 1978) (about how a boy spends one dollar since the previous Sunday) are both books with stories and mathematics that are inseparable and that complement each other. In contrast, there are no stories in the following counting books, which simply present pictures in which children can count objects if they so desire: *Count and See* (Hoban, 1972) (photographs of everyday objects), *Numbers* (Lippman, 1988) (a pop-up book), *The Wild-life 1,2,3* (Thornhill, 1989) (color illustrations of animals), and *1 Is One* (Tudor, 1956) (old-fashioned drawings).

A BOOK SHOULD FACILITATE
READERS' USE OF ITS MATHEMATICS

It is important to determine the extent to which a book provides an experience that will enable the reader to use, apply, transfer, or generalize its mathematics to new situations that might arise within daily life by:

> Presenting the story's characters in such a way that the reader would want to imitate their mathematical endeavors
>
> Providing adults who read the book to children with ideas or activities designed to extend its mathematics
>
> Encouraging the reader to extend its mathematical ideas by engaging in real-world experiments and activities
>
> Providing the reader with generalizations rather than only isolated facts

Presenting characters in such a way that readers want to imitate their mathematical endeavors is one way that books can facilitate application and transfer of their mathematics. Two examples illustrate this.

In *One More Thing, Dad* (Thompson, 1980) Caleb collects 10 items to take on a picnic and keeps track of them by counting on his fingers. The young reader easily identifies with Caleb and is likely to mimic his counting behavior both while reading the story and afterwards in real-life situations. In contrast, in *One Old Oxford Ox* (Bayley, 1977) (a collection of illustrated number tongue-twisters) and *I Can Count* (Bruna, 1968) (matched numbers and illustrations), there are no main characters for the reader to imitate and no overall stories that show how to use mathematics in one's life.

In *Around the Clock with Harriet* (Maestro & Maestro, 1984), Harriet (an elephant) gets a new watch that she uses to demonstrate to her friends both how to tell time and what time of day it is as she engages in her daily activities. She does so in a way that most children would identify with and want to imitate when they get their first watch. In contrast, *The Grouchy Ladybug* (Carle, 1977) shows 13 hours in the life of a very grouchy ladybug who does not use a time-telling device or show any awareness of clock time (even though a small clock shown on each page serves as a way of numbering the book's pages). As a result, the reader is not likely to imitate the non-existent mathematical behavior of the ladybug.

Children's books can also encourage children to apply, transfer, and generalize their mathematics by providing adults who read the books to children with "mathematical activities for children to engage in" and "mathematical ideas to talk about with children" at the front or back of the book. The activities can be either things for the child to engage in while reading the book (involving the use of the book) or things for the child to do after reading the book (involving the use of its mathematics). The "ideas to talk about" often provide the adult with ways of thinking about the book's mathematics that enable the adult to make a worthwhile contribution in a discussion with the child. Both types of suggestions are frequently called "notes to parents" or "notes to older readers." Examples of books containing activities for adults to have children engage in while reading are *Anno's Counting House* (Anno, 1982) (how to use pebbles while reading the book to clarify and generalize its mathematics) and *Anno's Hat Tricks* (Nozaki & Anno, 1985) (which provides adults with suggestions of both how to help children identify with the book's characters and how to help children think through its logic problems). Examples of books that contain activities for adults to have children engage in after reading are in all 12 books in the "Help Your Child Count Series" (Hales, Hales, & Amstutz, 1984), which include activities such as playing a board game, building towers with blocks, and counting candy. At the end of *How Much Is a Million?* (Schwartz, 1985), adults are told how its mathematics was calculated so that they can understand it sufficiently well to talk about it with a child. Many books without such notes could benefit from them. One example is *Alexander, Who Used to Be Rich Last Sunday* (Viorst, 1978) (the story about a boy who receives a dollar and spends it), which would be enriched by a short note to adults about how to help children use either paper-and-pencil calculations or real money to keep track of how much money Alexander has at the end of each of his monetary transactions.

Children's books can discourage readers from generalizing their mathematics by presenting them with an overwhelmingly large number of separate pieces of information. Examples of this type of book are *Measure with Metric* (Bradley, 1975) and *Angles Are Easy as Pie* (Forman, 1975).

THE RESOURCES NEEDED TO HELP READERS BENEFIT FROM A BOOK'S MATHEMATICS SHOULD NOT BE TOO GREAT

Sometimes an adult is needed to help a child benefit from a book's mathematics. If this is the case, a critical question is how much time, effort, and money an adult would need to expend in order to help a child benefit from a book's mathematics by

Rewriting, interpreting, highlighting, or explaining the book's mathematics if the mathematics is not appropriately highlighted or clearly
presented to the reader

Learning the book's mathematics (if the adult is unfamiliar with that
mathematics) in order to help the child understand that mathematics

Gathering specific materials that are required for use with the book

A child might not fully benefit from a book's mathematics if an adult does
not expend the necessary time, effort, or money needed to help a child understand it. There are three main reasons an adult may be unwilling to do so.

First, an adult might not be willing to expend the time and effort needed
to rewrite, correct, or highlight a book's mathematics if it is inadequately
presented. Examples of books' inadequacies abound in this chapter. Some
of them can be adjusted for easily; for example, an adult can easily ask a
child to count cookies and do the mathematics in *The Doorbell Rang*
(Hutchins, 1986). Other inadequacies, however, cannot be adjusted for so
easily. For example, the inadequacies of *The King's Chessboard* (Birch, 1988),
noted earlier in this chapter, are not easily overcome: It is difficult to correct
for the inaccurate and sloppy way in which measurement is treated and the
near invisibility of tables, graphs, or equations that present the story's mathematics. Almost all children's books can be rewritten for a child by an
accompanying adult who has the time, patience, and expertise to do so. When,
however, does the effort outweigh the benefits?

Second, the adult might be unfamiliar with a book's mathematics. Many
authors realize that not all adults will fully understand their book's mathematics or activities and so provide "notes to older readers" that explain the
mathematics, as discussed at the end of the previous section. Questions that
need to be asked about books are (1) should they have such notes? and (2) if
they do contain such notes, how well do the notes explain the mathematics
and how easily will the "typical" adult be able to understand them? This
latter question is important, for not all "notes to older readers" do an equally
good job of explaining their mathematics to adults.

Third, an adult may be unwilling or unable to gather the special materials needed for use with the book. Some books that require the reader to use
"things" are accompanied by the necessary manipulatives; others are not.
Some of these required but unprovided manipulatives are easy to acquire;
others are not. For example, many books on time suggest that readers make
a sundial. Compare the ease with which the materials can be obtained to
make the sundials described in the following books. *Time in Your Life* (Adler,
1955) requires the use of two flat pieces of wood (about 12 by 18 inches), a
dowel, several nails, a saw, a hammer, an atlas, a compass, a protractor, a
pencil, and a carpenter's level. *This Book Is About Time* (Burns, 1978) re-

quires the use of a pencil, a lump of clay or bubble gum, a piece of heavy paper or cardboard, a telephone book, and some tape. *The Clock We Live on* (Asimov, 1965) requires the use of a stake (or stick) driven (or stuck) into the ground. *Anno's Sundial* (Anno, 1985) requires only that the reader select the appropriate pop-up sundial from the book and pull it up from the page. The ease with which the materials can be obtained affects the adult's likelihood of acquiring or helping a child to acquire them.

CONCLUDING ISSUES

This chapter has presented mathematical and literary standards for evaluating children's mathematics trade books and discussed the mathematical standards with reference to selected children's books. In conclusion, five issues relevant to the use of such standards need to be briefly addressed.

First, it is critically important that a children's book containing mathematics should be a "good children's book." Given the scarcity of children's books containing mathematics, we are likely to use anything that exists on a particular mathematics topic—or publish anything that exists on such a topic. Unfortunately, poor literature may "turn kids off" to both mathematics and literature rather than stimulating their interest. Thus literary criteria, such as those in Figure 4.2, must be used when evaluating children's mathematics trade books.

Second, evaluation of children's books is a process of looking at books to "see" their strengths and weaknesses, and then judging what one has seen. Having several people examine a single book and share what they have seen and how they have made their judgments is extremely valuable for two reasons: It produces a more thorough and insightful evaluation of a book and it educates the evaluators so that they can both "see more" and "judge better" during future evaluations.

Third, when evaluating children's books it is often useful to examine several similar books at the same time. Being able to see how similar books measure up against the standards often gives great insight into the nature of individual books. In addition, a book should be evaluated not as an isolated entity but in the context of the body of literature out of which it grows and upon which its author (hopefully) aspires to improve.

Fourth, when evaluating a children's book it is often quite useful to ask how the book might have been written or illustrated in a more powerful way than it was, both from mathematical and literary perspectives. Seeing a book's potential, and how that potential might have been actualized (with either a small or large amount of effort), frequently provides a great deal of insight into a book's strengths and weaknesses—and what it has actually achieved (either in and of itself as an isolated work of art, or in comparison to books of a similar genre).

Fifth, educators who have critically evaluated children's mathematical trade books have consistently raised an important question: What do we do with the existing children's books that are mathematically flawed? This is the topic of Chapter 5. Suffice it to say that there are many things that can be done. Rather than throwing out books that do not meet the high standards suggested in this chapter, we can use those standards to identify their strengths and weaknesses—and then capitalize on their strengths and compensate for their shortcomings by enriching them in some of the ways described in the next chapter. Thinking about how to enrich children's books, and actually taking pen to book in order to implement the plans dreamed up, is one of the wonderful literary adventures in which both adults and children can engage.

5

Mathematical Enhancement of Children's Books

A major reason for using children's mathematics trade books is to help children have wonderfully enriching mathematical experiences while enjoying marvelously uplifting encounters with literature: to enable them simultaneously to explore mathematics and literature and to develop mathematical understanding, skills, and appreciations while also learning to understand, appreciate, respond to, and create literature.

To accomplish this, superb children's books are needed. Indeed, most of the literature about "how to use children's literature to teach mathematics" presents a view of children's books as wonderful, flawless items. However, educators who use children's trade books to teach mathematics frequently find the books lacking. Their mathematics can be incorrect, their mathematical ideas can be ineffectively presented or invisible to children, they may present an inappropriate view of mathematics, or they may involve children only minimally with the mathematics they contain. Thus educators are frequently caught between the idealistic vision of "what could be" (and, in fact, "what should be") and the reality of "what is."

Confronted with the less than perfect nature of children's mathematics trade books, educators often abandon books whose presentation of mathematics is inadequate. An alternative exists, however: to enhance the mathematical experiences that existing trade books present to children. They can be enhanced by children during mathematical literary criticism and editing; by teachers, librarians, parents, or other adults; or by their authors and editors in subsequent editions.

At least two different ways of enhancing the mathematics of children's books exist. One way is by embedding these books in a larger instructional context, which is the subject of a number of professional books (Braddon et al., 1993; Burns, 1992b; Kolakowski, 1992; Welchman-Tischler, 1992;

Whitin & Wilde, 1995). Likewise, Chapter 2 of this book—on mathematical literary criticism and editing—described one method of providing children with a wonderful mathematical and literary experience by the way in which a book is used during instruction. Yet another way of enhancing a children's book involves rewriting parts of it that are found to be lacking, a process based on assessing and understanding a book's story, its presentation of its story, its mathematics, the children who will encounter it, and one's goals for the book.

This chapter deals primarily with ways of mathematically enhancing children's books by rewriting parts of them. Many ways of doing so exist, and this chapter will discuss the following: using verbal clarifications and alterations, altering text, adding equations and algorithms, altering graphics, adding page extenders and end papers, inserting informational notes, adding physical manipulatives, changing a book's numbers, constructing question-and-answer flaps, inserting endnotes, and using magic slates.

FINDING A BOOK'S MATHEMATICS

In order to enhance a book's mathematics, one must first be able to find the mathematics. This relates to the mathematical standard (discussed in Chapter 4), "a book's mathematics should be visible to the reader." A person who is going to mathematically enhance a book must know where a book's mathematics is located and which of its mathematical topics are to be highlighted. This is frequently a more difficult task than it may seem, both because most of the children's books that are rich in mathematics contain many different topics that could be highlighted and because much of their mathematics is frequently hidden from view. Finding the mathematics in a book can be viewed as similar to playing "Hide and Seek" or "Treasure Hunt."

Most children's mathematics trade books provide a natural context for a mathematical treasure hunt that involves searching for, clarifying, articulating the meaning of, and checking the accuracy of their mathematics. If a book is read chapter by chapter, individuals can search each chapter for its mathematics. If working in a classroom setting, children can bring the results of their searches to the class as a whole for discussion. Frequently children and adults think that a book's mathematics does not make sense and are surprised to discover that it does, as is the case with the very strange and fantastic situations that lead to the invention of positive and negative numbers in *Charlie and the Great Glass Elevator* (Dahl, 1972). Conversely, children and adults frequently think that a book's mathematics does make sense and are surprised to discover that it does not, as is the case of *The Pushcart*

War (Merrill, 1964), which was written in the year 1986 and published in the year MCMLXIV (as discussed in Chapter 4). In such books the mathematical treasure hunt—the activities of searching for, clarifying, articulating, and checking the accuracy of a book's mathematics—becomes part of a continuing adventure that can enable children to see and appreciate the mathematics in their familiar everyday world.

If children and adults are engaged in a book's mathematical treasure hunt as part of a group, the issue frequently arises of how to share one person's discoveries about the location and meaning of mathematics without depriving others of the fun of discovering such themselves. In the beginning stages of such a treasure hunt, it seems appropriate to have some learners tell others where a book's mathematics is located. However, once mathematical literary critics have begun to discover mathematics in books and how to describe that mathematics in their own words, hints allow the critics to make these discoveries themselves, which is an important part of learning to be a powerful user of mathematics. Hints can be given about the location of a book's mathematics by simply indicating page numbers. Lists can also be compiled of pages that contain mathematics along with hints about the nature of the mathematics on each page.

VERBAL CLARIFICATIONS AND ALTERATIONS

Adults frequently compensate for books' inadequacies by making statements and provoking discussions while reading them to children. *The Doorbell Rang* (Hutchins, 1986) provides an example of how this can take place.

The Doorbell Rang is a story about sharing cookies. As shown in Figure 2.2, page 1 of the story has a picture of "Ma" putting a plate of 12 cookies on a kitchen table in front of two children, with the following text:

> "I've made some cookies for tea," said Ma.
> "Good," said Victoria and Sam. "We're starving."
> "Share them between yourselves," said Ma.
> "I made plenty."

On the next page, the text continues "'That's six each,' said Sam and Victoria."

On reading the first page of *The Doorbell Rang* to a child or group of children, an adult might ask "How many cookies are there on the plate?" to clarify how many cookies the "some" refers to. A discussion might follow during which a child counts the cookies. The adult could also ask whether the word *share* in this text means that each child needs to have the same number of cookies. Again, a discussion of this could follow. The adult could further ask how many cookies each child would get if they are to be divided equally and, perhaps, how this was discovered. Again, a discussion could follow, perhaps including a demonstration of how answers were obtained using physical manipulatives. All this verbal enhancement of the first page would clarify and highlight some of the book's mathematics and could take place before turning to the next page.

Here the educator who is reading the book orchestrates a discussion by asking questions and monitoring responses, something many teachers, parents, and librarians do as a natural and informal part of reading a book with children. The questioning and resulting discussion act as a mathematical enhancement to the book.

ALTERING TEXT

One of the easiest ways to enhance a book is by altering its text. *The Doorbell Rang* is an example of a book that could benefit from having its text altered and enriched both (1) to clarify some of its mathematical ideas and (2) to highlight some of its mathematical ideas so that they are more visible to the reader. Clarifying and highlighting mathematical ideas relates to the standards discussed in Chapter 4, particularly "a book's mathematics should be effectively presented" and "a book's mathematics should be visible to the reader."

One of the problems with *The Doorbell Rang* is that its story is so compelling and its mathematics so poorly highlighted that readers fly through the book wondering what will happen next, never noticing its mathematics. Another problem is that there is some ambiguity in its mathematical text. If children and adults identify these problems and think them worthy of being dealt with, they can be easily corrected. For example, the word *some* in the above text could be whited out and *12* written in its place or covered with a tab of paper with *12* on it (the tab of paper could be hinged on one side so a child could flip it up to see the original text, or glued down permanently). The word *equally* could be inserted (with an arrow and balloon or a caret) between the words *them* and *between* so that the line would read "Share them equally between yourselves." To increase the reader's mathematical involvement with the story, the following sentence could be placed at the bottom of the text: "How many cookies will each of you get?" The first page of the book with text would then read:

"I've made 12 cookies for tea," said Ma.
"Good," said Victoria and Sam. "We're starving."

"Share them equally between yourselves," said Ma.
"I made plenty."
"How many cookies will each of you get?"

After calculating the answer the reader would turn to the second page of the book to read, " 'That's six each,' said Sam and Victoria."

There are other ways of changing the text on the first page. Children have suggested using the word *dozen* instead of the number *12*, inserting the phrase *so each has the same number of cookies* after the word *yourselves* rather than using the word *equally*, or replacing the word *tea* with *snack*.

With a word processor, the words on a page could be reprinted using a font and type size similar to the book's and then pasted over the original words. Many teachers have successfully altered text in this way, in the hope that their alterations will not disrupt readers.

Too Many Eggs (Butler, 1988) provides another example of how a book can be enhanced by altering its text. Page 3 contains the following text:

With a large wooden spoon,
Mrs. Bear mixed together lots of sugar,
loads of butter, some honey, and
a mass of flour in a huge bowl.
How much sugar?
How much butter?
How much honey?
How much flour?
I do not know.
Mrs. Bear never, never counts
anything properly, because—
Mrs. Bear cannot count!

As pointed out early in Chapter 4, this is not a counting activity but one requiring measurements. However, the incorrect text provides a chance to identify and discuss the differences between counting and measuring, between using discrete and continuous materials when working with mathematics. These are critical distinctions for the person who is acquiring beginning number concepts. What better context to have them arise in than a children's book where author and editor alike have overlooked this significant distinction? The error is easy to correct—simply whiteout the words *counts* and *count* and substitute *measures* and *measure*. What mathematical power novice editors feel when they can make this simple correction. What an important perspective on word usage and the editing process the beginning writer has when the correction is made to the writing of a published author.

It is important for children and adults to realize that it is in their power to analyze a book's strengths and weaknesses, make a decision to improve a book by altering its text, and actually take pen to book to alter it. Changing the text in books is usually easy. Discovering that one has the power to do so is not always as easy to accept, particularly by adults, who sometimes believe that books are not to be "spoiled for others" by writing in them. However, that power is an important one for children and adults to experience if they are to become powerful users of mathematics who can discover mathematical problems in their world and solve those problems themselves—and if they are to become powerful literary critics or writers themselves. The skill and inclination to analyze and, where appropriate, alter one's own or another person's writing must be learned, and there is no more potent place for this learning to take place than in the context of clarifying and highlighting the meanings in a commercially published book.

ADDING EQUATIONS AND ALGORITHMS

Many books miss the chance to maximize the effectiveness of their presentation of mathematical ideas because they do not explicitly present the mathematical relationships underlying their stories by tactfully displaying numbers, equations, or algorithms that describe those relationships. Even when books do present such equations or algorithms, they frequently do not do so everywhere that it is appropriate. Children and adults delight in discovering this, often to the point of wanting to make explicit a book's mathematics to a degree that may seem to destroy its aesthetic elements by cluttering its pages with an overabundance of mathematics. Dealing with the issue of when too much mathematics is being placed on a page is, however, an issue that is best dealt with after novice editors have had some experience with putting mathematics on the pages of books.

Fat Cat (Hales et al., 1985) misses the chance to maximize the effectiveness of its presentation of mathematical ideas because it does not tactfully present numbers and equations in every appropriate place. *Fat Cat* is a story of a pirate captain (a fat cat) and her 9 crew members (rats) who act out the 10 addition number family—all the combinations of two whole numbers that add up to 10. The story is about how 9 rats must feed the cat to keep her from eating them and how the 9 hardworking rats free themselves from the cat. One two-page spread, which illustrates 4 pirates on one page and 6 on the other, reads as follows:

> On silent paws,
> while the captain snores,

three pirates wash the plates.
Then before she wakes
six make some cakes
to feed her for her tea.
   Four and six make ten.
   4 and 6 make 10 (pp. 9–10)

Here mathematical equations are conspicuously absent, as are numbers that indicate that there are four (4) crew members on the left-hand page and six (6) crew members on the facing right-hand page. Pictures illustrating the equation $4 + 6 = 10$, text illustrating this equation, and sentences paraphrasing this equation can easily be enhanced by simply writing the equation under the phrase "4 and 6 make 10" on the page, as is shown in Figure 5.1. Children and adults will also invent other ways of adding equations, some of which might involve the use of color. The process of discussing and reaching consensus about how to enhance a book's page, why the change is being made, and how the change clarifies or highlights the mathematics are important parts of making the change as well as important parts of individual development as mathematical and literary agents both for children and adults.

Alexander, Who Used to Be Rich Last Sunday (Viorst, 1978) is another book that does not present equations and algorithms in all appropriate places. This is a wonderful story about a boy who received a dollar the previous Sunday and quickly spent it. Nine monetary transactions take place as the book progresses, but nowhere in the book is a record kept of the amount of money that Alexander still has left to spend. (See Figure 5.2.) One way to use the book in published form is to read it once to children for their literary appreciation and then read it a second time and have children keep track of the amount of money Alexander has left at the end of each page by using paper-and-pencil algorithms, real money, or some other embodiment of money. Another way to enhance the book is to place an algorithm on each page depicting a monetary transaction, which accomplishes the following things: It enriches the story by allowing the reader to keep track of how much money Alexander has left after each monetary exchange; it makes the mathematics underlying the story visible to the reader; and it highlights for the reader how mathematics can be used in our everyday lives. Figure 5.3 shows one way an algorithm might be added to the upper-right-hand corner of page 15.

Considerations involved in deciding how to add an algorithm to the page include determining whether the answer to the problem should or should not be provided, whether integers with a cents sign or decimals with a dollar sign should be used, and whether the "scribbles" that accompany regrouping should or should not be depicted (and if so, in which format). Discussing

4 + 6

Then before she wakes
six make some cakes
to feed her for her tea.

Four and six make ten.
4 and **6** make **10**

4 + 6 = 10

On silent paws,
while the captain snores,
three pirates wash the plates.

FIGURE 5.1 Altered pages 9–10 of *Fat Cat*

FIGURE 5.2 Page 15 of *Alexander, Who Used to Be Rich Last Sunday*

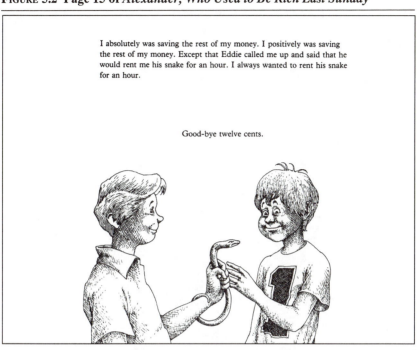

I absolutely was saving the rest of my money. I positively was saving the rest of my money. Except that Eddie called me up and said that he would rent me his snake for an hour. I always wanted to rent his snake for an hour.

Good-bye twelve cents.

these issues and making these decisions can lead children and adults to engage in quite a bit of mathematical communication, reasoning, and problem solving. For those with sharp eyes and intellects, the book offers many challenges, such as deciding if it is acceptable to depict an 8-cents coin. If it is not, issues arise about altering the book's graphics.

Perhaps the easiest way to add numbers to a book is to number its pages, which involves applying a mathematical algorithm to the pages of a book. (Many books, such as *The Doorbell Rang* and *Alexander, Who Used to Be Rich Last Sunday,* do not have their pages numbered.) Numbering a book's pages is an easy yet powerful act that greatly facilitates communication among those attempting to analyze and enhance a book.

For children and adults who enhance a book by adding numbers, equations, or algorithms, the wonderful mathematics experience lies not only in the production of the rewritten book but in the discussions engaged in and questions explored while searching for and discovering the book's strengths, its weaknesses, and ways to appropriately edit the book in order to compensate for its weaknesses and build upon its strengths.

FIGURE 5.3 Possible enhancement for the upper right corner of page 15 of *Alexander, Who Used to Be Rich Last Sunday*

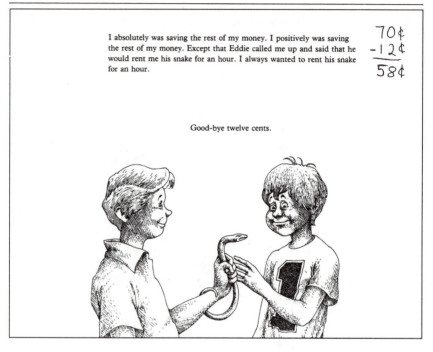

I absolutely was saving the rest of my money. I positively was saving the rest of my money. Except that Eddie called me up and said that he would rent me his snake for an hour. I always wanted to rent his snake for an hour.

$$\begin{array}{r} 70¢ \\ -12¢ \\ \hline 58¢ \end{array}$$

Good-bye twelve cents.

ALTERING GRAPHICS

Opportunities abound to highlight mathematics in children's books by imbedding it in their illustrations. It is unfortunate that books do not do so more frequently, given the ease with which this can be accomplished.

Examples of how to highlight books' mathematics by altering their graphics can be found in books that present the counting song "Roll Over." The first round of the song is

10 in the bed and the little one said:
"Roll over! Roll over!"
They all rolled over and one fell out.

In succeeding rounds the number 10 is decreased to 9, 8, 7, and so on down to 1. As discussed in Chapter 4, the song can be viewed as either a "counting down by 1" activity, which suggests including a number line to help children see where they are in the count from 10 to 1 and how each number relates to the others, or a "subtraction by 1" activity, which suggests inserting appropriate subtraction equations.

In *Roll Over! A Counting Song* (Peek, 1981), two facing pages are devoted to each round of the song: One presents the song and the other an illustration. Neither contains a number line or a subtraction equation. Figure 5.4 shows the book's first page and one way of inserting number lines in its bedposts and an equation in the footboard. Either enhancement would enrich the story.

Many other books about the song "Roll Over" exist, including *Roll Over!* (Gerstein, 1984), *Ten Bears in My Bed* (Mack, 1974), *Ten in a Bed* (Rees, 1988), and *There Were Ten in the Bed* (Adams, 1979). Each offers its own unique challenges for altering graphics. "Rewriting" one book does not diminish the learning that children might experience in rewriting a second or even third book about the same song. For example, because of its illustrations *Ten in a Bed* might best be thought of as a book about the "10 number family" rather than about "subtraction" or "counting back." In contrast, *There Were Ten in the Bed* might best be thought of as a book about "subtraction" because on each page of the book the reader actually removes one person from the bed, by turning a dial that rotates a person out of sight.

Anno's Mysterious Multiplying Jar (Anno & Anno, 1983) can be mathematically enhanced by altering the positions of the graphic components of its text and illustrations to allow them to present their information more effectively. This is a story about a mysterious jar that contains, among other things, 1 island that contains 2 countries, each of which contains 3 mountains, each of which contains 4 walled kingdoms, each of which contains 5 villages, each of which contains 6 houses, each of which contains 7 rooms, each of which contains 8 cupboards, each of which contains 9 boxes, each of which contains 10 mysterious jars like the one with which the story began. After presenting this sequence the story continues:

> Within each box there were 10 jars.
> But how many jars were in all the boxes together?
> The answer is surprising. There were 10! jars.
> But 10! does not mean just 10 jars.
> 10! means "10 factorial," or 3,628,800 jars. (p. 27)

The story then proceeds to explain what 10! means and why there are 10! jars. This is where graphic enhancement is needed.

FIGURE 5.4 **Page 2 of *Roll Over! A Counting Song* and a possible enhancement**

As discussed in Chapter 4, Anno first presents illustrations of the numbers 1! to 8!. They portray

1! = 1 × 1! = 1	by a dot rectangle	1 high by	1 wide
2! = 2 × 1! = 2	by a dot rectangle	2 high by	1 wide
3! = 3 × 2! = 6	by a dot rectangle	2 high by	3 wide
4! = 4 × 3! = 24	by a dot rectangle	4 high by	6 wide
5! = 5 × 4! = 120	by a dot rectangle	10 high by	12 wide
6! = 6 × 5! = 720	by a dot rectangle	24 high by	30 wide
7! = 7 × 6! = 5040	by a dot rectangle	70 high by	68 wide
8! = 8 ´ 7! = 40320	by a dot rectangle	140 high by	288 wide

The problem with this graphic portrayal is that the rectangles of dots do not follow a systematic pattern. If the rectangle of dots for 1! = 1 × 1! is *1* high by *1* wide, and 2! = 2 × 1! is 2 high by *1* wide, the dot rectangle for

3! = 3 × 2!	should be *3* high by	*2* wide (not 2 high by 3 wide)
4! = 4 × 3!	should be *4* high by	*6* wide (as it is)
5! = 5 × 4!	should be *5* high by	*24* wide (not 10 high by 12 wide)
6! = 6 × 5!	should be *6* high by	*120* wide (not 24 high by 30 wide)

Each of these rectangles fits on either a single page or two-page spread of Anno's book and preserves a pattern of numerical relationships in a way that highlights the nature of factorials. Each could be constructed on white paper and pasted over the book's existing rectangles. Of course the problem remains of what to do with 7!, 8!, 9!, and 10!. One could follow the model already set up by Anno and simply mention these factorials without illustrating them. Or the pattern could be verbally described in visual terms, perhaps by describing each factorial as a rectangle made up of dots of the following sizes:

7! =	7 dots high by	720 dots wide (which is | 10 pages wide)
8! =	8 dots high by	5040 dots wide (which is | 70 pages wide)
9! =	9 dots high by	40320 dots wide (which is | 560 pages wide)
10! =	10 dots high by	362880 dots wide (which is | 5040 pages wide)

Anno presents a second graphic description of factorials on page 40, shown in Figure 5.5. This table would be clearer if N! = N x (N – 1) ! was written out as N x (N– 1) x (N – 2) . . . 3 x 2 x 1 rather than 1 x 2 x 3 . . . (N – 2) x (N – 1) x N, so that the two forms of the equation are the same. (That is, in descending order of digits rather than ascending order, where 4! = 4 × 3! = 4 × 3 × 2 × 1 rather than 4! = 4 × 3! = 1 × 2 × 3 × 4.) It would also be clearer if all the 1's, 2's, 3's, and so forth, were lined up in a vertical col-

FIGURE 5.5 Anno's Factorial Table

```
 1! = 1x1! =                           1  =           1  (island)
 2! = 2x1! =                         1x2  =           2  (countries)
 3! = 3x2! =                       1x2x3  =           6  (mountains)
 4! = 4x3! =                     1x2x3x4  =          24  (walled kingdoms)
 5! = 5x4! =                   1x2x3x4x5  =         120  (villages)
 6! = 6x5! =                 1x2x3x4x5x6  =         720  (houses)
 7! = 7x6! =               1x2x3x4x5x6x7  =        5040  (rooms)
 8! = 8x7! =             1x2x3x4x5x6x7x8  =       40320  (cupboards)
 9! = 9x8! =           1x2x3x4x5x6x7x8x9  =      362880  (boxes)
10! =10x9! =        1x2x3x4x5x6x7x8x9x10  =     3628800  (jars)
```

umn rather than being located in diagonals that run across the middle of the table. Then, as shown in Figure 5.6, the reader could see more clearly how each succeeding factorial builds on the one before it, and the descending order of the digits in the factorial equation would correspond to the mathematical definition of factorials in the book.

The Doorbell Rang provides an example of how attention to graphic detail can provide opportunities to mathematically enhance a children's book.

Near the end of *The Doorbell Rang*, "Grandma" enters the kitchen with a large tray that has about 58 cookies on it. On the next page, Grandma has taken a few additional steps into the kitchen (and not yet removed her coat or set down her purse)—but she now has about 68 cookies on her tray. Mathematical literary critics delight in discovering this. This graphic inconsistency can be rectified by either redrawing the cookies on one of Grandma's trays or replacing both trays by a cookie jar.

A Grain of Rice (Pittman, 1986) can be mathematically enhanced by adding graphics to its story about a Chinese peasant, Pong Lo, who wants to marry the daughter of the emperor of China. After Pong Lo has saved the life of the princess, the emperor grants him any reward he wishes, except the hand of his daughter in marriage. Pong Lo requests that over a period of

FIGURE 5.6 Enhanced factorial table

```
 1! = 1x1! =                           1  =           1  (island)
 2! = 2x1! =                         2x1  =           2  (countries)
 3! = 3x2! =                       3x2x1  =           6  (mountains)
 4! = 4x3! =                     4x3x2x1  =          24  (walled kingdoms)
 5! = 5x4! =                   5x4x3x2x1  =         120  (villages)
 6! = 6x5! =                 6x5x4x3x2x1  =         720  (houses)
 7! = 7x6! =               7x6x5x4x3x2x1  =        5040  (rooms)
 8! = 8x7! =             8x7x6x5x4x3x2x1  =       40320  (cupboards)
 9! = 9x8! =           9x8x7x6x5x4x3x2x1  =      362880  (boxes)
10! =10x9! =        10x9x8x7x6x5x4x3x2x1  =     3628800  (jars)
```

100 days he be given a grain of rice the first day, double that amount of rice the next day, double that amount the next day, and so on for 100 days. The emperor grants this reward, without realizing the consequences. Pong Lo soon becomes the richest man in China and is about to drain the emperor of all his wealth, but he releases the emperor from fulfilling the reward when the emperor allows him to marry the princess. Mathematically, *A Grain of Rice* hinges on the seemingly "intellectually incomprehensible" way in which numbers become very large very quickly as a result of the doubling process—exponential growth is surprising to those who encounter it for the first time. Unfortunately, the book obscures its mathematics from the reader.

One way to enhance the book is by adding a graphic element that depicts how the number of grains of rice grow from day to day as the doubling process occurs. Simple, unobtrusive tables presented on pages where the number of grains of rice is spoken of would go a long way toward showing how the doubling process results in numbers growing large quickly. The tables would present data only for the number of days that had passed up until that point. Figure 5.7, which depicts such a table for day 20, shows the number of grains of rice given to Pong Lo on each of the first 20 days. Occasionally

FIGURE 5.7 Table for *A Grain of Rice*

Day	Grains of Rice
1	1
2	2
3	4
4	8
5	16
6	32
7	64
8	128
9	256
10	512
11	1,024
12	2,048
13	4,096
14	8,192
15	16,384
16	32,768
17	65,536
18	131,072
19	262,144
20	**524,288**

inserting small line graphs of this information could also provide a dramatic mathematical picture of what is occurring during the story.

A Grain of Rice could also be mathematically enhanced by changing its text. The book spells all of its numbers out in words. For example, "On the fortieth day, a caravan of one hundred elephants . . ." brought Pong Lo ". . . five-hundred-forty-nine-billion-seven-hundred-fifty-four-million-two-hundred-and-thirteen-thousand-eight-hundred-and-eighty-eight grains of rice" (pp. 50–52). Writing the number 549,754,213,888 in words may make it seem bigger because it is longer. However, using numerals—without the "ands"—instead of words would make *A Grain of Rice* more comprehensible.

ADDING PAGE EXTENDERS AND END PAPERS

There are books to which it is desirable to add information or graphics but whose pages are not the appropriate place to do so because the additions might disturb the integrity of the page, because they might overwhelm it, or because they are items that need to relate a set of pages to each other rather than simply enhance individual pages. Two ways of expanding beyond a page are by adding borders that extend beyond a page and by using the end papers and their facing pages inside the front and back covers of a book.

I'll Teach My Dog 100 Words (Frith, 1973), the story of a boy who teaches his dog 100 new words, could be mathematically enhanced by adding a few graphic components. The book needs graphic elements that tell readers which new words are being taught to the dog, indicate how many words have been taught up to a certain point, and visually portray the cumulative number of words taught up through any page in the book. New words taught to the dog could be highlighted by underlining them. The book already contains a numerical accumulator—a clipboard with a number being written on it—on 5 of the 15 two-page spreads that indicates how many new words have been taught up to that point; it could be drawn on the remaining two-page spreads as well. Most importantly, the book could benefit from a graphic element that visually portrays the cumulative number of new words taught up through any page. This could be accomplished by adding a border to the book's pages by taping a photocopy of a calibrated word meter (a 0-to-100 number track that would act like a rain gauge to indicate how many new words have been taught thus far) on the outer edges of each two-page spread (there is no room to add them within the pages without severely disrupting the graphic integrity of the book). The meter on the left side could indicate the number of new words taught prior to those pages, while the meter on the right side could indicate the number of new words taught through those pages. Figure 5.8 shows how these suggestions might be accomplished.

FIGURE 5.8 Possible enhancement for pages 2–3 of *I'll Teach My Dog 100 Words*

> The first six words
> I'll teach my pup
> are . . .
>
> dig a hole!

Page extenders could also be added to *The Doorbell Rang*, and teachers and children have done so in a number of different ways. One child added a page extender about 1-inch (2.5-cm) wide to the bottom of each of the book's pages. On it were drawn 12 cookies, spread out across facing pages. On each page where the cookies had to be redivided because new children entered the story, the appropriate number of cookies for each child was circled and a drawing of one of the children was placed next to each set of circled cookies thus neatly demonstrating the division of cookies.

A teacher added a page extender to the bottom of each of *The Doorbell Rang*'s pages to illustrate occurrences of addition and subtraction. On several of the page extenders a photocopy of the book's cat was placed on the left side of the page extender with a speech bubble emanating from its mouth. The cat said such things as "how many plates are on the table now?" and "plates on the table + plates in the cupboard = ?" Next to the cat were pictures and equations that depicted the distribution of 12 plates between the cupboard and table. Another teacher added a page extender to the bottom of each page that highlighted the pattern of shapes and colors on the floor, in the children's clothes, on "Ma's" skirt, on the table cloth, and in the border of the kitchen rug.

A third teacher added a page extender to *The Doorbell Rang* by mounting its pages on large pieces of construction paper that extended at least 4 inches (10 cm) beyond all the edges of the book. Comments about each page were then written on the page extenders. For example, the first page of *The Doorbell Rang* was extended as follows: On the page extender above the book's page, three cats have the following conversation. Cat 1 says, "Tea, yeck!! Why doesn't Ma serve milk or hot chocolate." Cat 2 says, "How many cookies are there on that platter?" Cat 3 responds, "Let's count them." On the extender to the side of the page the three cats have a conversation about sharing. Cat 1 says, "Does share mean that they each get the same number of cookies?" Cat 2 says, "Not unless Ma says to share equally!" Cat 3 responds, "Come on, Ma wants Victoria and Sam to share equally, even if she doesn't say so." On the page extender below the page the cats continue their conversation about sharing. Cat 1 says, "How can we find out how many cookies each child will get?" Cat 2 says, "I like the 'one for you and one for me' method. A first cookie for you, then a first for me. A second cookie for you and a second for me. And keep going until all the cookies are given out." Cat 3 responds, "I like to use the 'guess and equalize method.' You take 7 and I get 5. We compare and you have more, so you give me 1 and we compare again and see that we have the same." This type of enhancement allows the enhancer to stand back from the book and make comments about it, frequently at a metacognitive level. It also allows the book enhancer to model the type of thinking that is desirable for the reader to engage in.

The front and back end papers and the facing pages of *A Grain of Rice* (previously discussed) provide an ideal place to add graphic elements that summarize the book's ideas and relationships about exponential growth. The front papers could present an overview of its mathematical ideas before it begins (as an advance organizer) and the end papers could do the same after it ends (as a summary). The mathematical message could be summarized by placing tables, graphs, and/or illustrations that portray exponential growth and/or the relationship between the day number and the number of grains of rice received by Pong Lo on that day in the end papers of *A Grain of Rice*. Enhancers of this book might decide to use either one or multiple graphic elements to present the book's relationships: perhaps to show off what they know or perhaps because they want to show others that there are several different ways of representing the same mathematical relationships. Discussion about how to create an attractive graphic presentation of the book's relationships needs to be guided so that it becomes a consideration of the aesthetic dimensions of mathematics.

INSERTING INFORMATIONAL NOTES

Many books contain wonderful mathematics that is overlooked by readers—either because it is hidden, the momentum of the story inhibits the reader from stopping to do its mathematics, readers do not understand that mathematics is inherent in certain situations, or missing information makes it difficult to complete problems presented by a book—making it impossible for the reader to fully appreciate the meaning or humor of a book. Of concern here are the standards "a book's mathematics should be visible to the reader" and "a book should provide readers the information needed to do its mathematics."

The Pushcart War (Merrill, 1964) provides many examples of how bypassing a book's mathematics can deprive the reader of meaning that is critical to understanding it and its humor. The book is about a "war" between pushcart operators and truck drivers in New York City; each group wants to remove the other from cluttering the streets. On page 63, pushcart owners discuss what would happen if each of the 509 of them punctured 6 truck tires a day by shooting pins imbedded in peas shot from peashooters. The book simply notes that doing so would create many accidents. In fact, there would be 3,054 accidents a day, 21,378 accidents a week, and a stack of punctured tires more than 2 miles high each week. Much of the book's humor lies in the size of these numbers, but none of this can be comprehended unless the reader or book does the calculations. Later on the page the pushcart owners decide to buy a ton of peas and a ton of pins for their peashooters. How many is this? The book neither tells the reader or provides the reader with the necessary information to do the calculations. Readers could find the answer only if they actually weighed peas and pins and discovered that there are about 205 peas per ounce and 740 pins per ounce, meaning the pushcart owners are going to purchase about 4,920,000 peas and 17,760,000 pins! Here, too, the book's humor is linked to these large numbers. What are readers to do when confronted with missing information and hidden mathematics?

When confronted with missing information, readers can be guided to search it out. One group of fifth and six graders went to a grocery store and made some purchases when confronted with page 63 of *The Pushcart War*. They then weighed, counted, and calculated to discover the average number of peas (205) and pins (740) in an ounce and, from this, the estimated number of peas and pins in a ton. However, it is not always temporally efficient, monetarily economical, or administratively practical to have every child gather every bit of missing information.

Since the purpose here is to suggest ways that books can be mathematically enhanced, the focus is on finding ways that those who discover missing information can share it with others. One way is by writing notes in a book's margins that provide the missing information. Have you ever enjoyed reading someone else's notes in a borrowed library book? Have notes that you made in the margins of a book ever helped you understand the book better when you returned to examine it several days, weeks, or years later? Writing margin notes was once considered a scholarly art.

Margin notes can be used to provide missing information, ask questions, and demonstrate how to do problems—and all one needs to do is to write in the margins of books. Children or adults who write the notes can even sign their names to personalize them. Figure 5.9 illustrates one possible way in which margin notes might be added to page 63 of *The Pushcart War*.

A variation on this is to add enlarged margin notes by writing on a piece of paper slightly smaller than the size of the book pages and taping it to the edge of the related page, so that it can be folded into the book until the reader reaches the relevant page and opens it out to read it. The amount of information that can be added in this way is considerable. For example, one teacher enhanced *Alexander, Who Used to Be Rich Last Sunday* in this manner by inserting on each extended margin an illustration of Alexander's "diary," in which he kept track of the amount of money he had after each monetary transaction. Attached to the page on which Alexander rents Eddie's snake for an hour for 12 cents is an illustration of two pages of Alexander's diary. One page illustrates the equation and accompanying scribbling for $70¢ - 12¢ = ?$, and the other illustrates a note to himself in which Alexander wonders how much it would cost to rent the snake for 2, 3, 4, or 5 hours. Figure 5.10. shows how these diary notes might be added to the right hand side of page 15 of *Alexander, Who Used to Be Rich Last Sunday*.

Once the usefulness of informational notes is discovered, all sorts of "fun" ways of using them can be invented. Many children and adults like to insert them to convey to the reader "fun mathematical information" that is only tangentially related to a story. This was done with *The Doorbell Rang* when it was discovered that 2.4 billion pounds of cookies are commercially produced in this country each year. A note was inserted in white space on one of the book's pages in a 1-inch square box with a fancy border that stated, "Did you know . . . In the USA we make enough cookies for each person to eat one pound of cookies a month." The note was phrased this way after considerable discussion about what numbers were meaningful to 6-, 7-, and 8-year-olds, what were mathematically equivalent ways of saying that "2.4 billion pounds of cookies are commercially produced in this country each year," and what were the best ways of saying this. Here the mathematical and literary thinking engaged in by the authors of the informational note is as important as the note itself.

FIGURE 5.9 Possible additions to the margin of page 63 of *The Pushcart War*

paper. "If there are five hundred and nine pushcarts, and every man who has a pushcart—"

"And every lady," said General Anna.

"*And* every lady," agreed Maxie Hammerman. "If every pushcart peddler kills only six tires a day, that would be quite a few accidents."

"I am all for the accidents," said Frank the Flower, "but where can we get five hundred and nine pea shooters?"

"We will make them in my shop," said Maxie Hammerman. "Carlos' boy will show us how."

"Can we also make peas?" asked Papa Peretz.

"Peas, we can grow," said Eddie Moroney. "I have a window box, and already I have grown onions and beans good enough to eat."

"Good for you, Eddie Moroney," said General Anna. "But I am not going to wait for peas to grow in your window box. Much less to dry out. We must attack at once."

"We can buy the peas," said Harry the Hot Dog.

"Yes," said Maxie Hammerman. "I will order one ton of peas in the morning."

"And a ton of pins," said General Anna.

"A ton!" said Mr. Jerusalem. "But how much will so many pins cost? Even scrap metal junk by the ton—it adds up. I should know. Scrap metal is my line. And one ton of new high-quality pins—who can afford? Not to mention one ton of peas, also an expense."

"Pin money we will need," Maxie Hammerman agreed. "And I will get it."

63

Margin notes:

How many killed tires a day?
How many killed tires a week?

How much money will be needed?

How many peas in a ton?
How many pins in a ton?
Does this make sense?

experiments show that there are about 205 peas in an ounce 720 pins in an ounce

an ounce of pins cost $.25 peas cost $.15

16 ounces = 1 pound 2,000 pounds = 1 ton

FIGURE 5.10 Possible enhancement for the right side of page 15 of *Alexander, Who Used to Be Rich Last Sunday*

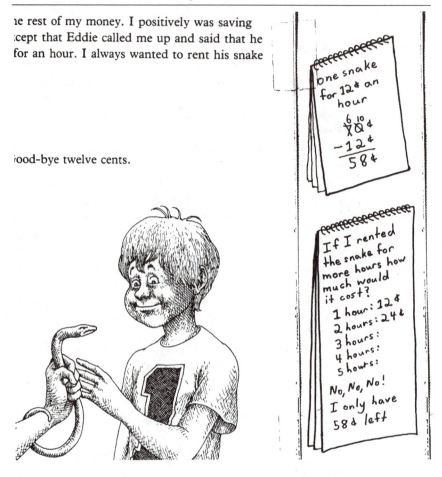

ıe rest of my money. I positively was saving

:cept that Eddie called me up and said that he

for an hour. I always wanted to rent his snake

ıood-bye twelve cents.

ADDING PHYSICAL MANIPULATIVES

The use of physical manipulatives to help children see mathematical meanings, understand mathematical concepts, and acquire mathematical skills is suggested in the research literature and recommended by the National Council of Teachers of Mathematics. It is not difficult to add simple physical manipulatives with instructions for their use to a children's trade book, nor is doing so something new.

Many books involving time concepts contain cardboard clocks with movable hands. For example, *What Time Is Grandma Coming?* (Seymour,

1983) and *It's About Time* (Anastasio, 1993) both contain circles that are cut through all of their pages to show the inside back cover, which contains a clock with movable hands that is centered in the die-cut circles so that the clock can be used on each page of the books. Both books sell for under $10.00. *My First Book of Time* (Llewellyn, 1992) has a cardstock fold-out flap that contains a clock with movable hands that the reader can use adjacent to each of the pages of the book. *The Time Book* (Cassidy, 1991), which cost $10.95 in 1993, comes with a working wristwatch. Some books that deal with symmetry come with mirrors, such as *Make a Bigger Puddle, Make a Smaller Worm* (Walter, 1971) and *"M" Is for Mirror* (Birmingham, 1988). Some counting books come with manipulatives, such as *Too Many Eggs* (Butler, 1988) (which comes with eggs printed on die-cut cardstock that the reader punches out and uses while reading the book) and *Count with Little Bunny* (Ziefert & Campbell, 1988) (which contains a sheet of reusable die-cut colorform plastic stickers that are torn out of a piece of flexible plastic and then temporarily affixed to its plastic coated pages by the reader to aid in the counting process). Other books, such as *Ten Beads Tall* (Adams, 1988), come with centimeter cubes attached to a string for use in measuring items in the book. The technology even exists to print inexpensive calculators into the covers of books.

With a little imagination, a wide variety of books can be mathematically enhanced by adding manipulatives for children to use while doing the books' mathematics and, where necessary, instructions on how to use them.

Alexander, Who Used to Be Rich Last Sunday (Viorst, 1978) can be easily enhanced by attaching a packet of play money for children to use while reading it. Children can first read it solely to appreciate the story and then read it a second time, pausing after each monetary transaction to act it out and see how much money Alexander has left. If this is done, a decision has to be made about what to put in the packet of money. If the goal is to introduce or review the value of different coins, then one will want to use pennies, nickels, dimes, quarters, and a dollar bill. If the goal is to model with coins the written subtraction algorithm that describes the monetary exchanges that take place, then one will want to use only pennies, dimes, and a dollar bill. (The subtraction algorithm most frequently used is based on the place-value nature of our base-10 number system, with its trades of 10-for-1 between columns. No trades are ever recorded in this number system involving groups of 5 or 25.) While the decision of which coins to put in the money packet may at first seem trivial, it is of crucial importance because it reminds us that one's goals for a book can dramatically affect how it is enhanced. One cannot decontextualize the enhancing of a children's book. The author, editor, and mathematical enhancer of a children's book are always operating in a curricular, instructional, literary, social, and epistemological context where goals make a difference.

Inch by Inch (Lionni, 1960), another book that can be enhanced by adding physical manipulatives, is the story of an inchworm (that is actually an inch long in its illustrations) that must survive the hunger of several birds by measuring a robin's tail, a flamingo's neck, a toucan's beak, a heron's leg, a pheasant's tail, a whole hummingbird, and a nightingale's song. The inchworm survives because of its ability to measure and its ability to engage in problem solving.

It can be easily enhanced by attaching either an inexpensive tape measure or a packet of 1-inch cubes, which children can use to measure the birds. Which manipulatives are used depends on the goals of the book enhancer and the mathematical knowledge of the children for whom the book is intended.

Three issues arise when children measure the birds in *Inch by Inch*. First, the robin's tail is not 5 inches long, as the book states, but about 3 inches long, an inaccuracy children will need to deal with. Second, children will want to measure other birds in the book and communicate their inquiries to other readers. Determining how to add text and record the results of experiments using language that is consistent with that of the story is a major editorial endeavor. Third, children will raise issues related to the scale of the birds: Are the birds and bird parts depicted in the book the actual size that they are in real life? In other words, is a hummingbird really about 3½ inches long? If it is not, is a robin's tail about the same length as a hummingbird? These are important questions about scale for children to reflect upon.

These issues concerning *Inch by Inch* point out something important that occurs when a reader does a book's mathematics by using manipulatives rather than by simply observing the mathematical endeavors of a book's characters. When children simultaneously read a book and actually do its mathematics, they are frequently simultaneously involved in several complementary mathematical endeavors. In the case of *Inch by Inch*, children simultaneously engage in the activities of problem posing, problem solving, reasoning, measuring, seeing the applicability of mathematics in the real world, dealing with issues of scale, dealing with issues of measurement inaccuracies, and learning to challenge answers provided to mathematical problems by other persons. Engaging in multiple mathematical endeavors simultaneously and seeing the cumulative impact of their interactions is one of the things that helps children feel mathematically powerful.

Physical manipulatives can be used to enhance *The Doorbell Rang*. The most obvious way is simply to include manipulatives that represent cookies and plates in a Ziploc bag that is attached to the book, but with a little imagination it is possible to go beyond this. One teacher laminated the pages of the book and used cookies made out of stickees that children could move about on the pages of the book. (Stickees are vinyl reusable stickers that easily adhere to and can be removed from laminated surfaces.) Other teachers have made abundant use of Velcro.

Enhancing books by adding physical manipulatives to them relates to the mathematical standard "a book should involve the reader in its mathematics." By including play money, an inexpensive tape measure, or play cookies with a book, the book suddenly has the potential of allowing the reader to do its mathematics rather than simply to observe the mathematical endeavors of its characters. Mathematically enhancing a book to allow a reader to become a doer rather than simply an observer of mathematics is a significant accomplishment. The old poem that states "I hear and I forget, I see and I remember, I do and I understand" only points out the finding of a considerable body of research about how children learn mathematics, research that highlights the importance of actually becoming physically and intellectually involved in doing mathematics as compared to hearing or reading about someone else's endeavors. This message is equally true for children's construction of literary meaning: The degree to which a child can become physically, emotionally, and intellectually involved in experiencing, understanding, critically reflecting upon, and creating literary meaning is likely to be directly related to the amount that a child will learn from an encounter with a book.

CHANGING A BOOK'S NUMBERS

Sometimes children read a trade book they love but whose mathematics is inappropriate because it violates the standard "a book's mathematics should be intellectually and developmentally appropriate for its target audience." An example of this type of inappropriateness is found in *How Much Is a Million?* (Schwartz, 1985), a book with illustrations and story appropriate for lower elementary grades but with mathematics appropriate for upper elementary grades. At other times a book's mathematics is "inappropriate" because there is little correspondence between its numbers and those found in children's everyday world.

Alexander, Who Used to Be Rich Last Sunday (Viorst, 1978) is a book that can be enhanced by changing its numbers to make them more appropriate. Why change the numbers? The most compelling reason is that children who engage in mathematical literary criticism and editing have commented that getting $1 from your grandparents during a visit is no big deal. Somewhere between $5 and $20 has been suggested as a more appropriate gift. In addition, children have said both that most of the things they would like to purchase would cost more than 20 cents (the largest monetary transaction in *Alexander*) and that the cost of items in the book is far less than what the items would cost in a store. One way of overcoming these difficulties is by changing its numbers as a result of determining the relationship between the cost of the items in the book and the cost of the items in a local store. One class of fourth graders discovered that multiplying all numbers in the book by 5 transforms them into amounts that are reasonable for 1995. As a result of a school survey they also discovered that most elementary school children would be happy receiving a gift of $5 from their grandparents.

The Philharmonic Gets Dressed (Kuskin, 1982) is a book that a class of sixth graders decided needed to be changed. The book is about how the 92 men and 13 women of a philharmonic orchestra get ready for a performance. It begins with the members of the orchestra taking baths or showers; proceeds to describe how they get dressed, how they get to the performance hall, how they prepare their instruments and warm up; and then shows them performing. A sample of one passage indicates the richness of the book's mathematics:

> When all the men have their underwear on, they get into long-sleeved white shirts and button them up. Then they put on black trousers. Forty-five men stand up to get into their pants. Forty-seven sit down. Each pair of pants has a shiny black stripe down the outside of each leg. (pp. 37–38)

What was upsetting to the sixth graders about *The Philharmonic Gets Dressed* was the ratio of men to women. Several members of the class did research to find out the ratio of men to women in different orchestras, and then decided that they did not like this ratio. The class decided what they thought the appropriate ratio should be and then changed all the numbers in the book to reflect their preferred ratio.

Mathematics problem solving is often viewed as an endeavor that deals with immutable and unchangeable numbers that are given to the problem solver by an adult, book, or the real world, but the numbers we deal with do not have to be viewed as unchangeable. Budding mathematicians and editors can be socially conscious, they can decide that the ratios of different types of persons within a book are not what they should be, and they can change those ratios when they enhance a book. The ratio of males to females, children to adults, handicapped to nonhandicapped persons, persons of different skin color, persons of different hair color, or persons with different-priced clothing can all be calculated for a particular book, for a particular community, or for a nation. Those ratios can guide the enhancement of a book, or they can be intentionally ignored and other ratios used instead. Using mathematics and language together can help us understand our world, it can help us envision a different (and perhaps more just or more comfortable) world, and it can help us to communicate our vision to others. Budding mathematical editors discover some of the power of mathematics and language when they see that mathematics and language do not have to describe only what was or what is but can also be tools that project a vision of what might be.

CONSTRUCTING QUESTION-AND-ANSWER FLAPS

Many authors seem to have difficulty posing a mathematical problem for readers and providing an answer in such a way that the reader can solve the problem before looking at its answer. Some solve this difficulty by putting the answer on the next page as part of the story. Some put the answer in the back of their book. Others do not provide answers at all. Many simply put answers on the same page as the problems, eliminating the possibility of children's engaging in problem-solving activity. Some avoid stating a problem where one exists and simply provide the answer to an unstated problem. (This occurs frequently in counting books, where the question "How many items are on this page?" is never posed even though the answer is dramatically provided.) At issue is the question of how to pose a mathematical problem to readers and provide the answer to that problem on the same page without giving away the answer.

Where's Spot? (Hill, 1980) is a simple book for preschoolers about such geometrical concepts as inside and outside, behind and in front, under and above. It poses questions to the reader and puts their answers underneath flaps. To the query of whether or not Spot is hiding behind the door, the reader is presented with a paper door that can be opened to see the answer underneath. Other flaps include the door of a grandfather clock that can be opened (for inside), the top of a piano that can be raised (for in), and a rug that can be lifted up (for under). Question-and-answer flaps allow answers to problems posed on a page to be hidden from the readers until after they have a chance to solve the problems.

Alexander, Who Used to Be Rich Last Sunday is a book in which question-and-answer flaps can be used. The book does not present the reader with a record of Alexander's monetary transactions, so the reader does not know how much money Alexander has at different times during the story. Earlier we discussed how problems could be added to the book in order to remedy this situation. The difficulty with those solutions is that they either present the problem without its answer, so the reader has no way of knowing the correct answer with certainty, or they present the problem with the answer, thus depriving the reader of the fun of solving the problems. Question-and-answer flaps eliminate this difficulty. A piece of paper about 3 inches

(8 cm) high by 1 inch (2.5 cm) wide can be folded in half to form a flap about 1½ inches (4 cm) high, the problem corresponding to the monetary transaction can be written on the outside, the algorithm and answer can be written on the inside, and then the flap can be glued down to the page. Once the reader solves the problem on the flap's outside, the flap is raised to see the answer underneath. Figure 5.11 shows how such a flap might be constructed and attached to the upper-right-hand corner of page 15 of *Alexander, Who Used to Be Rich Last Sunday*. Note that the small spiral note pad in Figure 5.10 could be transformed into a question-and-answer flap by using a note pad page that could be lifted to see what was underneath.

Often answers to problems posed are prominently displayed in such a way as to deprive readers of the chance of solving the problem. *Time to . . .* (McMillan, 1989) provides an example of this. Each two-page spread in the book contains, among other things, a photograph of a clock on a boy's bedroom wall, the clock's time displayed digitally (7:00 A.M.), and the time of day spelled out with words (as in "seven o'clock in the morning"). If the

FIGURE 5.11 Possible addition to the upper right corner of page 15 of *Alexander, Who Used to Be Rich Last Sunday*

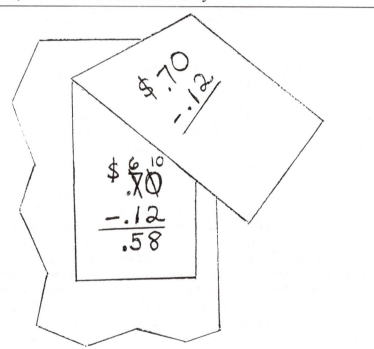

mathematical enhancer of *Time to . . .* wishes to cover up the digital representation of time (for example, the "7:00" in "7:00 A.M.") and the verbal representation of time (for example, the "seven" in "seven o'clock in the morning") so that the reader must "read the clock" to tell what time it is, this is easily accomplished. All that needs to be done is to construct question flaps to cover the answers that are already printed in the book. To do so one need only cut out a rectangular piece of paper slightly larger than the words and numbers, fold and score it about one-fourth of an inch (.5 cm) along the side that is to be pasted to the book, and then paste the smaller part of the flap onto the book in such a way that the larger portion covers the desired material. Often one need not even write a question on a question flap if an appropriate symbol (such as a picture of a digital clock) is placed on the flap. Cardstock, such as that found in index cards, often works better than paper.

There are many other types of question-and-answer flaps. One worth mentioning is the letter-in-envelope flap, first widely publicized in *Griffin & Sabine* (Bantock, 1991), which consists of a letter placed in an envelope that is glued or taped to a page of a book. A question or problem is written on the outside of the envelope, and the letter can be removed from the envelope to discover the book enhancer's thoughts. This form allows the book enhancer to elaborate in a more lengthy manner than a simple flap does. A question such as "Can you find three ways to solve the problem presented on this page?" might yield six or seven different types of solutions in a letter, something that could not fit under a simple flap. Diagrams, graphs, and maps are often more suitably placed in an envelope than under a flap. Of course, there is no reason why a letter needs be long; the small note cards and envelopes that florists and confectioners send with gifts can easily be pasted into books.

Another type of question-and-answer flap is the sliding answer tab with a window, which is made of two pieces of cardstock: a cover and a paddle. (Index cards work well for this.) The cover, with a window cut in it and a question written on it, is pasted onto a page of a book only at its edges, with one edge left partially open. The other piece of cardstock is cut in the shape of a paddle so that it can slide back and forth under the other piece of cardstock when the handle of the paddle is pulled. The paddle has the answer written on it. The handle of the paddle sticks out of the unglued part of the cover; when it is pulled, the answer on it slides into the window of the cover so that the person pulling the paddle can see the answer to the question on the cover through its window. Figure 5.12 portrays a sliding answer tab designed to be used with *The Doorbell Rang*. Many variations on the sliding answer flap exist. Some have multiple windows and paddles; others have a circular cover and a paddle that is rotated. *The Math Kit* (Van Der Meer & Gardner, 1994) presents multiple variations on this type of device.

FIGURE 5.12 Sliding answer tab for *The Doorbell Rang*

Cover with window. Apply glue to
crosshatched edges.

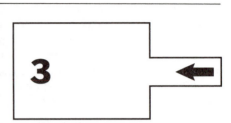

Paddle with answer.

Paddle inserted under cover.

INSERTING ENDNOTES

Endnotes are informational notes or problems at the end of a book for
the reader to ponder after a book has been read. At least three different types
of endnotes can contribute to the mathematical enhancement of a children's
book: those that elaborate for "older readers" a book's mathematics so that
they can discuss it with a child after the book has been read; those that suggest activities for the younger reader that extend the book's mathematics into
the child's everyday world (these can be directed to children or adults); and
those that pose mathematical problems to the child that turn the child's attention back into the book to examine its mathematics in greater depth. All three
types of endnotes exist in currently published books.

Anno's Mysterious Multiplying Jar (Anno & Anno, 1983), for example,
has an endnote for older readers that describes factorials and how they are
useful in understanding the book's story as well as arranging desks in a classroom. *The King's Commissioners* (Friedman, 1994) contains an endnote for
adult readers that discusses both its mathematics and how children learn
mathematics.

Roll Over! (Gerstein, 1984) provides adults with the music and words to the song that the book is named after, so that adults can sing the song with children. *Fat Cat* (Hales et al., 1985) tells adults how to extend the book's ideas with things to do with children: playing with water toys, using a box of 10 toys to simulate the ship within the story, and enacting a pretend production of the story.

In contrast, *Counting on Frank* (Clement, 1991) has two different types of endnotes, both of which are addressed to young readers: One type poses mathematical problems to young readers to turn their attention back into the book to reexamine it in order to gain greater appreciation of its mathematics and story; another type extends the investigations begun in the book beyond it into children's everyday world. *Counting on Frank* is about a boy who loves to do mathematics and his dog, Frank. The boy investigates such things as how long a line a ballpoint pen will draw before running out of ink (7,000 feet) and how many of his dog, Frank, will fit in his bedroom (24). The endnotes tempt readers to do mathematics related to the book's story through reference to objects either within the story or within the child's everyday world. For example, the reader's attention is turned back into the book when one of the endnote questions asks:

> Frank's "pet boy" calculates that twenty-four Franks could fit into his bedroom. What if, in addition to these twenty-four Franks, thirty Franks could fit into the boy's parents' bedroom, twenty-five in the living room, ten in the bathroom, and twenty in the kitchen? How many Franks in all would fit into the boy's house? (n.p.)

The reader's attention is turned toward the everyday world when the following endnote activity is suggested:

> Have a counting contest with your friends or family. Fill a measuring cup with dry macaroni noodles. Can you guess how many noodles it takes to fill the cup? Write down everyone's guess and count the noodles to see who is closest to being right. (n.p.)

Attaching endnotes to books is not difficult. A variety of different types of endnotes might be appended to *The Doorbell Rang* (Hutchins, 1986). The young reader's attention might be extended beyond the book by providing a recipe for no-bake chocolate chip cookies to build measurement skills or turned back to the book's mathematical problems by asking how many cookies each child would receive if the cookies that Grandma brought were added to the cookies that Ma baked. Older readers might be offered a mathematical perspective on the book and activities to extend the interest generated by the book through a discussion of different ways in which the book's division problems can be solved and suggestions about ways that children could perform the story as a play.

Endnotes to *Alexander, Who Used to Be Rich Last Sunday* (Viorst, 1978) could easily describe the use of a variety of physical manipulatives. For older readers, an endnote might describe "chip-trading" games that use a money till, dice, and either play money, poker chips, or base-10 blocks. This note might also describe the benefits of different types of place value manipulatives, the types of difficulties that children have when doing monetary calculations involving subtraction, other children's books that deal with the mathematics of money, and a variety of other types of boardgames that involve the use of money (such as Monopoly). For younger readers, an endnote might suggest that the reader act out the story using money, to focus them back on the book's mathematics. An endnote for younger readers that focuses them on their everyday world might ask them to write short stories with themselves as the main characters in which they receive $20 that they must spend on items advertised in their Sunday newspaper.

It should be noted that research has shown that if parents and teachers are given a choice between the same children's mathematics trade book that either contains or lacks (tactfully presented) endnotes, they most frequently choose the book with endnotes (Halpern, 1994). Books can contain frontnotes, which are directions, information, or problems (usually provided to an older reader) that are to be read before a children's book itself is read; they usually consist of directions for how to read or use a book.

USING MAGIC SLATES

While enhancing *Alexander, Who Used to Be Rich Last Sunday*, a teacher had an idea: Why not laminate the pages of the book so that children would not ruin them with repeated use? She discovered that children could write on the laminated pages with a crayon and the writing could later be removed with a cloth. Laminating the pages turned them into magic slates. Another teacher then adapted this idea with the same book by designating a writing space on each page on which there was a monetary transaction, a boxed area where the children were to keep track of the monetary transactions in the book. These were inserted prior to laminating the pages of the book. In the procedure she developed, the children first read the book for enjoyment. Then they read the book a second time, calculate the amount of money Alexander has after each monetary transaction, and write the amount on the magic slates in the designated places. The children then check their work with a calculator and show it to the teacher. Finally, they wipe off the crayon marks with a cloth.

Since these first experiments with magic slates many teachers and children have created and used a variety of magic slates with a wide range of books. Sometimes they laminate only a small part of the page of a book. Sometime they use clear contact paper rather than a laminating machine. Sometimes they use erasable markers rather than crayons, markers that are attached to the book with a ribbon or piece of string. Sometimes the magic slates are put on top of question-and-answer flaps with the answers underneath. Sometimes the magic slates are created on pieces of cardstock that are separate from the book and attached to the book by a piece of string. One teacher put a magic slate in a pocket that was glued onto a page in a book so the slate could be removed to do a calculation on that page. Magic slates are enhancements that children enjoy using, that motivate them to do book's calculations, and that are easy to implement.

OTHER WAYS OF ENHANCING BOOKS

Many other ways of enhancing books exist. They include posing problems to readers and hiding answers in pop-up devices, on origami creations, within fold-out pages, or by using mirror writing; putting items in baskets that are carried throughout a book for use in acting out a story; and inserting songs to be sung either after a book is read or at special times during the reading of a book.

Books can also be enhanced by personalizing them. At the simplest level, this involves changing the names of a book's characters to those of the children who will read the book, their friends, relatives, teachers, or other relevant persons. At a more complicated level, this can involve inserting new events into a book that the children will be familiar with because of their own recent experiences (for example, unique events that recently occurred on a field trip or at recess).

A far richer mathematical and literary experience is created if books are enhanced while working in groups engaged in mathematical literary criticism and editing than if an individual works alone.

CRITICAL CONCLUDING ISSUES

Some of the ways of capitalizing on the strengths and compensating for the inadequacies of children's mathematics trade books by mathematically enhancing them have been discussed in this chapter. In conclusion, five issues need to be addressed.

First, is it possible to put too much mathematics in a children's book?

The answer is clearly "Yes!" The goal should be to provide children with wonderfully enriching mathematical and literary experiences, not simply to stuff as much mathematics as possible into books. The mathematical enhancement of a book must be done in such a way that it enriches the book and does not detract from its story. The goal is to draw out of its story its mathematical ideas so that the story becomes richer and more interesting.

Second, is there any evidence that children will enjoy mathematically enhanced books more than the original versions? Research clearly indicates that children prefer stories with enhanced mathematics over the original stories—when the enhancements are tactfully executed. When a teacher gave them a choice of taking home a mathematically enhanced version of a trade book or an unenhanced version of the same book, after both versions had been read to them, children overwhelmingly preferred to take home the enhanced version (Halpern, 1994).

Third, persons who engage in mathematical literary criticism and editing and who enjoy mathematically enhancing children's trade books often reach the point of asking, "Can I do a better job of writing children's books that contain mathematics than many others who have written such books in the past?" The answer to this question is, quite simply, try to find out. Over 3,000 children's books are published a year. Yours might be one of them.

Fourth, it might be asked whether the methods of enhancing books suggested in this chapter could be used in areas other than mathematics. For example, can children's trade books containing science or history be enhanced in similar ways to those described in this chapter? The answer is "Yes!" The applications of the ideas presented in this chapter are limited only by the reader's imagination.

Fifth, one might worry that the enhancements presented in this chapter will slow down the pace at which a reader is capable of reading a book. Readers frequently read a book by simply skimming along the trail of words left by the author, without questioning or actively engaging the text encountered. This is not the type or reading that is desired by book enhancers, who want children to stop skimming type. They want to interrupt the reader so that the reader will think about what is occurring in the book. A much more active role for the reader is intended, during which the reader is challenged to stop, encounter problems, make meaning, and think about what is occurring in a book. As a result, many of the enhancements presented in this chapter interrupt the speedy flow of words within a book and challenge the reader to actively take a second look at what was said, what was not said, what was pictured, or what occurred on the pages of a book.

Appendix

REPRODUCTION INSTRUCTIONS

If the assessment instrument in this appendix is used to evaluate books, it should first be reproduced in such a way that it is enlarged to a size that fits on a standard 8½-by-11-inch sheet of paper. Enlarging by about 35%, depending on the reproduction machine, should result in the correct page size.

LIMITED REPRODUCTION PERMISSION

CHILDREN'S MATHEMATICS TRADE BOOKS:
EVALUATION FORM
by MICHAEL SCHIRO

Reviewer:_____   Date: _____

Book name:	
Author:	Publisher & Date:
Short description of plot or theme:	
Mathematics content presented:	Target Audience (circle all appropriate): preschool K 1 2 3 4 5 6 7 8 9

Answer the following, based on responses on the subsequent pages of this instrument.

How good is the book, from a mathematical perspective?	5 superb	4	3 average	2	1 worthless
How good is the book, from a literary perspective?	5 superb	4	3 average	2	1 worthless

What are the book's best mathematical features?
What are the book's worst mathematical features?
What are the book's best literary features?
What are the book's worst literary features?

Based on your responses above, rate the book:

How good is the book?	5 superb	4	3 average	2	1 worthless

GENERAL COMMENTS:

Mathematical Standards

Is the book's mathematics correct and accurate?	5 correct	4	3 inaccurate	2	1 incorrect
Comments:					

Is the book's mathematics effectively presented?	5 effectively	4	3 average	2	1 poorly
Comments:					

Is the book's mathematics worthy of being learned?	5 worth learning	4	3 questionable value	2	1 not worth learning
Comments:					

How visible to the reader is the book's mathematics?	5 optimally	4	3 partially	2	1 not visible
Comments:					

Does the book present an appropriate view of mathematics?	5 optimally appropriate	4	3 partially appropriate	2	1 not appropriate
Comments:					

Is the book's mathematics intellectually and developmentally appropriate for its audience?	5 optimally	4	3 partially	2	1 unsuited
Comments:					

How involved does the reader get with the book's mathematics?	5 very	4	3 average	2	1 minimally
Comments:					

Does the book provide the information needed to do its mathematics?	5 fully	4	3 partially	2 insufficient	1	☐ N/A
Comments:						

Do the book's story and mathematics complement each other?	5 complement	4	3 no effect	2	1 detract
Comments:					

Does the book facilitate readers' use, application, transfer, and generalization of its mathematics?	5 help	4	3 neutral	2	1 inhibit
Comments:					

How great are the resources needed to help readers benefit from the book's mathematics?	5 minimal	4	3 average	2 excessive	1	☐ N/A
Comments:						

Literary Standards

Plot: Is the book's plot or story well developed and imaginative, flowing logically, believably, and sensibly from one idea to the next?*	5 4 3 2 1 ☐ excellent poor N/A
Comments:	

Characterization: Are the book's characters well portrayed and believable?*	5 4 3 2 1 ☐ excellent poor N/A
Comments:	

Style: Does the book contain a vivid and interesting writing style that actively involves the child?	5 4 3 2 1 excellent poor
Comments:	

Language: Does the book use correct grammar and punctuation and age-appropriate language and style?	5 4 3 2 1 excellent poor
Comments:	

Readability: Is the book's knowledge content and readability appropriate to the age of the reader ?	5 4 3 2 1 excellent poor
Comments:	

*This category is primarily relevant to storybooks; if not applicable, mark N/A.

Interest: Is the book's interest level relevant and developmentally age-appropriate to the reader?	5 4 3 2 1 excellent poor
Comments:	

Enrichment: Does the book enrich the child by enhancing or increasing the child's developmental level?	5 4 3 2 1 excellent poor
Comments:	

Graphics: Are the book's illustrations, pictures, or graphics well chosen, appealing, text-relevant, and representative of a child's view of the world?	5 4 3 2 1 excellent poor
Comments:	

Unity: Do the book's plot, content, and/or graphics convey the same stylistic message?	5 4 3 2 1 excellent poor
Comments:	

Respect: Does the book's tone respect the reader, do characters provide positive role models who are culturally diverse and free from stereotype?	5 4 3 2 1 excellent poor
Comments:	

Physical Traits: Is the book visually appealing, well organized, durable, and laid out to produce easy comprehension?	5 4 3 2 1 excellent poor
Comments:	

Notes

Chapter 1

1. Sheila Egoff (1973), a literary expert, believes that about 2.5% of all children's books are excellent, 62.5% are mediocre, and 35% are extremely poor. Examination of four critical annotated bibliographies that evaluate children's mathematics trade books yields very different results. The Indiana State Department of Public Instruction's *Annotated Bibliography of Children's Literature Related to the Elementary School Curriculum* (1979) rated 49% of its 187 entries as highly recommended and 51% as recommended. Of the 186 books evaluated in *Children's Mathematics Books: A Critical Bibliography* (Matthias & Thiessen, 1979) 31% were deemed highly recommended, 23% recommended, 42% acceptable, and 5% not recommended. *The Wonderful World of Mathematics: A Critically Annotated List of Children's Books in Mathematics* (Thiessen & Matthias, 1992) rated 23% of its 493 entries as highly recommended, 29% as recommended, 44% as acceptable, and 4% as not recommended. In *Counting Books Are More Than Numbers: An Annotated Action Bibliography,* Roberts (1990) looked at 460 books and rated 17% of them as recommended; the remaining 83% were left without a recommendation.

2. When the evaluative criteria used in the bibliographies mentioned in note 1 were carefully examined, they were found to be quite primitive. A literature review turned up only four additional items that addressed the issue of how to evaluate children's mathematics books: Ballenger, Benham, & Hosticka (1984); Farr (1979); Harsh (1987); and Strain (1969). Only Ballenger and associates presented a rigorous set of evaluative criteria, which were only for one of the "general" areas in which they believed children's counting books should be assessed.

Chapter 3

1. Many of us are familiar with the literary benefits of reading something two or three times—the advantages that derive from checking to see if we have read correctly and understood appropriately the first time, and the benefits of being able to better understand a story as a result of already knowing what it is about and to delve deeper into the meaning of specific events because we know their place within the entire story. In the language arts, these benefits are frequently discussed. However, professional writing on the connection between mathematics and children's literature rarely recommends reading a story or passage more than once and provides few examples of educators doing so.

References

Adams, P. (1979). *There were ten in the bed*. Singapore: Child's Play.

Adams, P. (1988). *Ten beads tall*. Singapore: Twinn.

Adler, I. (1955). *Time in your life*. New York: John Day.

Anastasio, D. (1993). *It's about time*. New York: Grosset & Dunlap.

Anno, M. (1982). *Anno's counting house*. New York: Philomel.

Anno, M. (1985). *Anno's sundial*. New York: Philomel.

Anno, M. (1986). *Socrates and the three little pigs*. New York: Philomel.

Anno, M. (1987). *Anno's math games*. New York: Philomel.

Anno, M. (1989). *Anno's math games II*. New York: Philomel.

Anno, M., et al. (1986). *All in a day*. New York: Philomel.

Anno, M., & Anno, M. (1983). *Anno's mysterious multiplying jar*. New York: Philomel.

Asimov, I. (1965). *The clock we live on*. New York: Abelard-Schuman.

Ballenger, M., Benham, N., & Hosticka, A. (1984). Children's counting books. *Childhood Education, 61*, 30–35.

Bang, M. (1983). *Ten, nine, eight*. New York: Scholastic.

Bantock, N. (1991). *Griffin & Sabine*. San Francisco: Chronicle.

Baroody, A. J. (1993). *Problem solving, reasoning, and communicating*. New York: Macmillan.

Baumann, H. (1976). *The hare's race*. New York: Morrow.

Bayley, N. (1977). *One old Oxford ox*. New York: Atheneum.

Bettelheim, B. (1976). *The uses of enchantment: Meaning and importance of fairy tales*. New York: Knopf.

Birch, D. (1988). *The king's chessboard*. New York: Dial Books.

Birmingham, D. (1988). *"M" is for mirror*. Norfolk, England: Tarquin.

Braddon, K. L., Hall, N. J., & Taylor, D. (1993). *Math through children's literature: Making the NCTM standards come alive*. Englewood, CO: Teacher Ideas Press.

Bradley, F. M. (1975). *Measure with metric*. New York: Crowell.

Brown, S., & Walters, M. (1983). *The art of problem posing*. Hillsdale, NJ: Erlbaum.

Bruna, D. (1968). *I can count*. London: Methuen.

Burk, D., Snider, A., & Symonds, P. (1991). *Math excursions 2*. Portsmouth, NH: Heinemann.

Burns, M. (1978). *This book is about time.* Boston: Little, Brown.

Burns, M. (1992a). *About teaching mathematics.* Sausalito, CA: Math Solutions.

Burns, M. (1992b). *Math and literature (k–3).* Sausalito, CA: Math Solutions.

Butler, C. M. (1988). *Too many eggs.* Boston: Godine.

Carle, E. (1977). *The grouchy ladybug.* New York: HarperCollins.

Cassidy, J. (1991). *The time book.* Palo Alto: Klutz.

Chase, N. D., & Hynd, C. R. (1987). Reader response: An alternative way to teach students to think about text. *Journal of Reading, 30,* 531.

Clement, R. (1991). *Counting on Frank.* Milwaukee: Gareth Stevens.

Cuisenaire Company of America. (1991). *Cuisenaire catalogue, k–9.* White Plains, NY: Author.

Dahl, R. (1972). *Charlie and the great glass elevator.* New York: Knopf.

De Garmo, C. (1895). Most pressing problems concerning the elementary course of study. In C. A. McMurry (Ed.), *First yearbook of the Herbart Society.* Normal, IL: Pantagraph, Print, and Stationery Co.

Eeds, M., & Wells, D. (1989). Grand conversations: An exploration of meaning construction in literature study groups. *Research in the Teaching of English, 23,* 4–29.

Egan, K. (1986). *Teaching as story telling: An alternative approach to teaching and curriculum in the elementary school.* Chicago: University of Chicago Press.

Egoff, S. (1973). If that don't do no good, that won't do no harm: The uses and dangers of mediocrity in children's reading. *Issues in Children's Book Selection: A School Library Journal Anthology* (pp. 4–5, 7). New York: Bowker.

Elkin, B. (1957). *Six foolish fishermen.* New York: Scholastic.

Emberley, E. (1973). *Ed Emberley's little drawing book of the farm.* Boston: Little, Brown.

Farr, Pamela L. (1979). Trends in math books for children. *School Library Journal, 26,* 99–104.

Forman, R. (1975). *Angles are easy as pie.* New York: Crowell.

Friedman, A. (1994). *The king's commissioners.* New York: Scholastic.

Frith, M. K. (1973). *I'll teach my dog 100 words.* New York: Random House.

Frye, N. (1963). *The educated imagination.* Toronto: Canadian Broadcasting Corporation.

GEMS. (1993). *Once upon a GEMS guide: Connecting young people's literature to great explorations in math and science.* Lawrence Hall of Science, University of California, Berkeley.

Gerstein, M. (1984). *Roll over.* New York: Crown.

Griffiths, R., & Clyne, M. (1991). *Books you can count on: Linking mathematics and literature.* Portsmouth, NH: Heinemann.

Hales, R., Hales, N., & Amstutz, A. (1984). [Help Your Child Count Series]. London: Granada.

Hales, R., Hales, N., & Amstutz, A. (1985). *Fat cat.* London: Granada.

Halliday, M. A. K. (1975). *Learning how to mean: Explorations in the development of language.* London: Edward Arnold.

Halpern, P. (1994). *The effects of enhancing the mathematics in children's trade books.* Unpublished doctoral dissertation, Boston College, Chestnut Hill, MA.

Hardy, B. (1977). Towards a poetics of fiction: An approach through narrative. In M. Meek, A. Warlow, & G. Barton (Eds.), *The cool web: The pattern of children's reading* (pp. 12–23). New York: Atheneum.

Harsh, A. (1987). Teach mathematics with children's literature. *Young Children, 42,* 24–29.

Hill, E. (1980). *Where's Spot?* New York: Putnam's.

Hinton, J., & Rafferty, S. (1990). *Kindercorner math: Linking children's books to math.* Littleton, MA: Sundance.

Hoban, T. (1972). *Count and see.* New York: Collier.

Hoogeboom, S., & Goodnow, J. (1987). *The problem solver 3: Activities for learning problem solving strategies.* Sunnyvale, CA: Creative Publications.

Hunt, P. (1991). *Criticism, theory, and children's literature.* Oxford: Blackwell.

Hutchins, P. (1986). *The doorbell rang.* New York: Mulberry.

Indiana State Department of Public Instruction. (1979). *An annotated bibliography of children's literature related to the elementary school mathematics curriculum.* Indianapolis: Indiana State Department of Public Instruction.

Jennings, C. M., Jennings, J. E., Richey, J., & Dixon-Krauss, L. (1992). Increasing interest and achievement in mathematics through children's literature. *Early Childhood Research Quarterly, 7,* 263–276.

Johnson, M. (1990). *When I learn to tell time.* New York: Gallery.

Kelly, P. R., & Farnan, N. (1991). Promoting critical thinking through response logs: Reader response approach with fourth graders. In J. Zutell & S. McCormick (Eds.), *Learner factors/teacher factors: Issues in literacy research and instruction* (pp. 277–284). Chicago, IL: National Reading Conference.

Kilpatrick, W. H. (1918). *The project method.* New York: Teachers College Press.

Kliman, M. (1993). Integrating mathematics and literature in the elementary classroom. *Arithmetic Teacher, 40*(6), 318–321.

Kolakowski, J. S. (1992). *Linking math with literature.* Greensboro, NC: Carson-Dellosa.

Kubler, A. (1988). *Albert moves in.* Swindon, England: Child's Play.

Kuskin, K. (1982). *The philharmonic gets dressed.* New York: HarperCollins.

Lionni, L. (1960). *Inch by inch.* New York: Scholastic.

Lippman, P. (1988). *Numbers.* New York: Grosset & Dunlap.

Llewellyn, C. (1992). *My first book of time.* New York: Dorling Kindersley.

Lovitt, C., & Clarke, D. (1992). *The Mathematics Curriculum and Teaching Program* (MCTP)*: Professional development package activity bank* (Vol. 2). Carlton, Victoria: Curriculum Corporation.

Mack, S. (1974). *Ten bears in my bed.* New York: Random House.

Madison, J. P., & Seidenstein, R. (1987). *Beyond numbers: The mathematics literature connection.* Reston, VA: The Mathematics Education Trust.

Maestro, B., & Maestro, G. (1984). *Around the clock with Harriet.* New York: Crown.

Many, J. E., & Wiseman, D. L. (1992). The effect of teaching approach on third grade student's response to teaching literature. *Journal of Reading Behavior, 24*(3), 265–287.

Mathews, L. (1978). *Bunches and bunches of bunnies.* New York: Scholastic.

Matthias, M., & Thiessen, D. (1979). *Children's mathematics books: A critical bibliography*. Chicago: American Library Association.

McGee, L. M. (1992). Focus on research: Exploring the literature-based reading revolution. *Language Arts, 69, 529–537.*

McGrath, B. (1994). *The m&m's counting book*. Watertown, MA: Charlesbridge Publishing.

McMillan, B. (1986). *Counting wildflowers*. New York: Lothrop, Lee & Shepard.

McMillan, B. (1989). *Time to . . .* New York: Lothrop, Lee & Shepard.

Merrill, J. (1964). *The pushcart war*. New York: Dell.

Moerbeek, K., & Dijs, C. (1988). *Six brave explorers*. Los Angeles: Intervisual Communications.

Nasco. (1995). *Nasco Math '95*. Modesto, CA: Author.

National Council of Teachers of Mathematics (NCTM). (1989). *Curriculum and evaluation standards for school mathematics*. Reston, VA: National Council of Teachers of Mathematics.

Nozaki, A., & Anno, M. (1985). *Anno's hat tricks*. New York: Philomel.

Parker, R., & Goodkin, V. (1987). *The consequences of writing: Enhancing learning in the disciplines*. Upper Montclair, NJ: Boynton/Cook.

Peek, M. (1981). *Roll over! A counting song*. New York: Houghton Mifflin.

Pittman, H. C. (1986). *A grain of rice*. New York: Hastings House.

Planet Dexter. (1995). *How high is pepperoni?* Reading, MA: Addison-Wesley.

Polya, G. (1957). *How to solve it*. Princeton, NJ: Princeton University Press.

Rees, M. (1988). *Ten in a bed*. Boston: Little, Brown.

Roberts, P. L. (1990). *Counting books are more than numbers: An annotated action bibliography*. Hamden, CT: Library Professional Publications.

Rosenblatt, L. M. (1938). *Literature as exploration*. New York: Noble & Noble.

Rosenblatt, L. M. (1978). *The reader, the text, the poem: The transactional theory of the literary work*. Carbondale: Southern Illinois University Press.

Rosenblatt, L. M. (1991). Literature—s.o.s. *Language Arts, 68, 444–448.*

Sachar, L. (1989). *Sideways arithmetic from Wayside School*. New York: Scholastic.

Scarry, R. (1975). *Richard Scarry's best counting book ever*. New York: Random House.

Schwartz, D. M. (1985). *How much is a million?* New York: Scholastic.

Sendak, M. (1962). *One was Johnny*. New York: Harper & Row.

Seymour, P. (1983). *What time is grandma coming?* Los Angeles: Intervisual Communications.

Sheffield, S. (1995). *Math and literature (K–3): Book two*. Sausalito, CA: Math Solutions.

Sitomer, M., & Sitomer, H. (1970). *What is symmetry?* New York: Crowell.

Sloan, G. D. (1991). *The child as critic* (3rd ed.). New York: Teachers College Press.

Slobodkina, E. (1987). *Caps for sale*. New York: Scholastic. (Original work published 1940)

Snyder, T. (1991). *The wonderful problems of Fizz & Martina*. Cambridge, MA: Tom Snyder Productions.

Stariano, P. (1994). *Storytime math: Math explorations in children's literature.* Palo Alto, CA: Dale Seymour Publications.

Strain, L. B. (1969). Children's literature: An aid in mathematics instruction. *Arithmetic Teacher, 16,* 451–455.

Thiessen, D., & Matthias, M. (1992). *The wonderful world of mathematics: A critically annotated list of children's books in mathematics.* Reston, VA: National Council of Teachers of Mathematics.

Thompson, S. L. (1980). *One more thing, Dad.* Chicago: Albert Whitman.

Thornhill, J. (1989). *The wildlife 1,2,3.* New York: Simon & Schuster.

Tudor, T. (1956). *1 is one.* Chicago: Rand McNally.

Van Der Meer, R., & Gardner, B. (1994). *The math kit.* New York: Scribner's.

Viorst, J. (1978). *Alexander, who used to be rich last Sunday.* New York: Atheneum.

Vygotsky, L. S. (1978). *Mind in society: the development of higher psychological processes* (M. Cole, Ed.). Cambridge, MA: Harvard University Press.

Wahl, J., & Wahl, S. (1976). *I can count the petals of a flower.* Reston, VA: National Council of Teachers of Mathematics.

Walter, M. (1971). *Make a bigger puddle, make a smaller worm.* New York: Evans.

Walter, M. (1985). *The mirror puzzle book.* Norfolk, England: Tarquin.

Webster's new collegiate dictionary. (1991). Springfield, MA: Merriam-Webster.

Welchman-Tischler, R. (1992). *How to use children's literature to teach mathematics.* Reston, VA: National Council of Teachers of Mathematics.

Whitin, D. J., & Wilde, S. (1992). *Read any good math lately: Children's books for mathematical learning.* Portsmouth, NH: Heinemann.

Whitin, D. J., & Wilde, S. (1995). *It's the story that counts.* Portsmouth, NH: Heinemann.

Ziefert, H., & Ernst, L. C. (1988). *Count with little bunny.* New York: Viking.

Index

About the Author

Michael Schiro teaches courses in mathematics education and curriculum theory at Boston College, where he coordinates programs in elementary education. He received his doctorate from Harvard University, is an inventor of games, has taught in urban schools, and does research in the areas of curricular integration and the ways in which educators' philosophies evolve over the span of their careers.